NETWORKING THE KINGDOM

To
Pat + Rosemarie,
My
good
Friends
in
dance!

Pals forever
Jay

1-4-96

O.J. BRYSON

NETWORKING THE KINGDOM

A Practical Strategy for Maximum Church Growth

WORD PUBLISHING
Dallas · London · Vancouver · Melbourne

NETWORKING THE KINGDOM

All Scripture quotations, unless otherwise noted, are from The Everyday Bible, New Century Version. Copyright © 1987, 1988 by Word Publishing, Dallas, Tex.

ISBN 0-8499-3238-6

0 1 2 3 9 RRD 9 8 7 6 5 4 3 2 1

Printed in the United States of America

To
Hetty Sue Bryson
Our sister
Say "Hi" to Mom

So the two men went with Jesus. . . . One of the
men was Andrew. . . . The first thing Andrew
did was to find his brother, Simon. . . . The next
day Jesus . . . found Philip. . . . Philip found
Nathanael and told him.

John 1:39–45

T E A M
/Jesus
/Andrew
/Peter
/Philip
/Nathanael
/You
/Me
/Neighbor

Contents

v

Acknowledgments

In a way, *Networking the Kingdom* is a "family affair." It is a result of relationships in my own family as well as my extended family of networkers everywhere. Each family brought its own influence.

I would like to say thanks to Dr. Jewell Bryson for introducing me to the Geyser Basin at Yellowstone and for serving as an advisor and proofreader. Thanks to Ralph Bryson for proofreading, and for biblical text guidance. Ralph and Jewell are two of my brothers.

It was Scott Bryson, my oldest son, who helped pull the germ idea from me and who had more to do with helping it to germinate than any human; he was also a good sounding board.

Chris Bryson, my youngest son, located the Scripture references and patiently listened as I bounced every idea off him.

Thanks to my other brothers and sisters for all they gave to me when there was not that much to give.

A special thanks to Stephanie Brown for her editorial work. This was her second book with me.

Thanks to all those ministers and other staff members who have given me guidance in many ways as the concept was being birthed. Also, thanks to Peg Brennan for proofreading the manuscript.

To those who opened the door to networking for me, thanks. To those in my network, for whom it was my privilege to open the door, I owe much. I honor you who are in networking everywhere, as you are continuing to open the door.

Preface

On January 25, 1989, little did I know that I would meet a man who would help me find the missing link in helping my church grow. On Wednesday of the Fourth Dimension Business Luncheon, I met Dr. O. J. Bryson. We shared some small talk and went our separate ways.

When I returned to the office, I asked my secretary to set up a luncheon with Dr. Bryson. A few days later we met for lunch.

I began to share with him my frustration about reaching people. In our conversation, I shared how I had traveled all across the nation speaking to thousands of people, and yet for some reason, it was difficult to reach people in this location.

I told him that when I came to this church, it was in a steady decline in membership, losing about sixty to eighty members a year for the previous ten years. On top of that, the church would soon be one hundred years old. For this church to grow, it would almost have to deny all church growth principles. The community was not a fast-growing community, and we had an older congregation in a very traditional setting.

We had begun to develop some new strategies for growth. But we were having a problem reaching people. We could not afford to do a lot of advertising because the church was facing financial difficulties. Honestly, I had just about given up.

I shared this with Dr. Bryson, and his eyes lit up like a light bulb. He said, "I think I can help you." Then he got out a napkin and began to write down the Team Seven strategy on networking. It took a few minutes, and then it sunk in. I quickly realized our greatest asset was "people reaching people" and penetrating their networks.

Because I had served on the South Carolina and the Texas Evangelism Division, I had some of the best training available in reaching people. But I realized we had missed the most important element. That missing element was reaching someone, and then helping that person reach his network of friends.

When a person comes into our churches, it doesn't take long before he loses touch with his "unchurched friends." He is now surrounded by "churched friends." Team Seven gave me a handle on how to help these new people coming into our church reach their friends and help the new friends' friends reach their friends.

The thing that excited me as much as anything was the fact that we did not have to change anything. I had already been through some tough times, because every new thing I would introduce meant some change. It was refreshing to know that in this concept (Team Seven), nothing had to change. We simply used available people to reach their network of friends.

I think Team Seven could be the greatest tool the church has seen since Jesus sent the disciples out, two by two, to reach the masses with the Gospel. Team Seven is so simple. It disturbs me when I realize how many years it has taken us to discover what I believe is the easiest, most natural, and most productive way of reaching people. I thank God for Dr. O. J. Bryson and his keen insight into *Networking the Kingdom*.

Rev. Knox Talbert, Pastor

Foreword

The most significant thing I see in Team Seven is that it gives the church the chance to reach people where they are, at their own levels and locations, instead of forcing them immediately to conform to the church's environment.

Even though the gospel is being preached in many places, often it is not understandable to the unchurched. Team Seven gives us the chance to speak to people in their language, on their turf.

Sound waves are flying through the air constantly, but until they reach my eardrum, I can't hear them. Once the eardrum picks up the vibrations, I can then translate these sounds into something I can understand. That's how the gospel is. Until people are in a location where they can hear it, and until it is in a language they understand, it's just meaningless noise. Remember the miracle of Pentecost.

I heard a speaker tell the story of a photographer for sky-divers. He was the best in his field. He was liked and loved by everyone. All the sky-divers wanted him to film their jumps because he would jump with them.

One day he dove out of the plane without his parachute and tragically fell to his death. Everyone wondered in horror, how could someone as good as he forget his parachute?

He had a lot of important things on his mind. He had to remember his camera and film. He had to tell everyone, and himself, exactly when to jump, and in what sequence. He had to get everyone to remember in what sequence he would shoot the scenes as the sky-divers performed their aerial acrobatics. He had his mind on what colors to wear that would show up against the sky. He was the best. He remembered everything except the most important thing. He forgot his parachute and fell to his death.

A church may remember to do many important things. But if it forgets the main thing, reaching people, the church "falls to its death." Team Seven helps the church to do the main thing.

Scott Bryson, Student

Introduction

If their plan comes from men, it will fail. But if it is from
God, you will not be able to stop them. You might even be
fighting against God himself!

—Acts 5:38–39

There's a popular song about having only words to use,
but we don't have anything but words, either, do we?
I'm a businessman and not a theologian, so please judge my
words in that light.

Because I am from the mountains of east Tennessee, I still
retain most of my mountain ways and dialect. People seldom accuse me of being from London. One scholar said to
me one day, after first hearing me talk, "I've discovered the
unknown tongue."

I studied five languages in graduate school, but I am still
a hillbilly at heart. Now that may sound a little braggado-
cios to you, but since my background is surely going to be

exposed as I reveal more and more of myself to you, I wanted you to at least know I am an educated hillbilly.

I need to do just a little bit more bragging. Once upon a time I was the Assistant Blackberry Salesman for the Frog Pond Hollar Briar Patch. My sister Wilma and I sold the berries beside the highway that went from Cleveland to Ocoee, Tennessee. It was an honorary position, as she had appointed me to be her assistant. I bet you never thought God would be sending you a message from a briar patch in Frog Pond Hollar, Tennessee.

If we are going to be spending this much time together, we ought to get to know each other. So let's just sort of talk our way through this as if we were down at the coffee shop.

I need to take care of one little bit of business before we get too far along. This is called a DISCLAIMER:

> No one can guarantee that the techniques and approaches suggested in this material will work for you. I hope, however, that the ideas presented here will assist you in growing a great church or organization, or in developing a strong, profitable business.

The Lull Before the Storm

This part is the lull before the storm, because as soon as we get to know each other a little, I am going to jump in with both feet, and you are going to have to hold on. I won't waste one word, or one moment of our time.

I'm just an average salesman, but I'm an above average teacher. You may not accept everything I say, but you won't have any trouble understanding me. When I get through, you'll either be sad, glad or mad. My goal is to make you a little of all three:

1. Glad that I told you about Team Seven.
2. Sad that you didn't know about it sooner.
3. Mad at the Devil for any reason you can think of.

When I sold Bibles door to door in college for the Southwestern Company, they taught us a concept: "Any fool can criticize, and most fools do." We can't say that to our church members when they criticize, can we?

Because what I have to say to you is important, I am anxious to please, and not to offend you. Well, I am not as anxious to please you as I am to see that I don't offend you. But more important than that, I can't afford to get you noticing me so much that you miss what I am trying to say to you. David said:

> I hope my words and thoughts please you.
> Lord, you are my Rock,
> the one who saves me.
> —Psalm 19:14

If I seem a little tentative here at the beginning, it is because we don't quite know each other yet, and I am trying to get to know you, and to get you to like me a little before we start. There's something else, too. Some of the people who are going with us on our little adventure (it may not be so little by the time we get through) are business people and some are church staff members. So no cussin'.

I have reason to be nervous, because I am attempting to communicate here with leaders from all different faiths. You will recall that some of the bloodiest battles in history were fought because people got cross-ways on certain differing religious points of view. I know of a church that ran the pastor off because he switched the piano to where the organ was and the organ to where the piano was. No. I don't know why he did it. I used to, but I can't remember. But he doesn't pastor there anymore. I think he remembers why.

Centuries ago, the Baptist denomination split, and one of the big causes was a dispute over whether or not to have "hymn singing" as opposed to "Psalm singing" in the church.

I'm trying to talk to you as a businessman about the use of Team Seven in the church without saying anything that would cause a doctrinal controversy.

If I were a clergyman, I would probably have used only Scripture quotes, but since I am a businessman, I have tossed in a little salt and pepper in the form of quotes and sayings from famous people. I use these to drive home a particular point, especially in the area of developing people skills.

Some may find that offensive. If so, they may have been "too far inside," too long. They may need to "stand by the door" a while. (That story is in chapter 11.) The writer of the Book of Proverbs said he was right in the middle of the congregation, and he wouldn't listen. He said,

> [I] have not obeyed the voice of my teachers,
> nor . . . them that instructed me.
> I was almost in all evil
> in the midst of the congregation. . . .
> —Proverbs 5:13–14 (King James Version)

There was another fellow who had the same problem which is: How is the best way to communicate my teachings? It was a long time ago, but his thoughts came out more eloquently than mine. So if it's okay, I'll borrow his. I know you're ahead of me, and you think I am talking about "Put your snout in the Gospel spout,/And get it lit up with Him." But that's not the one I'm talking about.

J. S. Bach, one of the two greatest composers of the baroque period, found a torch song from his day and harmonized the tune; someone set a fellow's words to it, and it became a classic. I share only one verse, but I think it's the most beautiful single verse in all of hymnody. See what you think:

> What language shall I borrow
>   To thank Thee, dearest friend,
> For this Thy dying sorrow,
>   Thy pity without end.
> O make me Thine forever;
>   And, should I fainting be,
> Lord, let me never, never
>   Outlive my love for Thee.[1]

As custodian of the Team Seven concept, I wish there were a special "language" I could "borrow," that would help me communicate across denomination lines, so that each of you would receive the same message: Team Seven is a way He can reclaim His unto Himself, and we can help do it.

But all I have are words—my words. All you and I have going for us are my words, your sincere interest, and a request to Him for His guidance.

That's not enough. At least it's not enough if you and I can't communicate. I can't take you if you won't go. If I mess up and make you mad, His Spirit may be quenched, and we may never get together. We've got to make do with you and me and Him. That's enough if we can get along. If I do hurt your feelings, you've got to forgive me. Blame it on my background, and then become a little more thick-skinned and a little more soft-hearted.

I need your patience when you see through my theological weaknesses. To find a flaw in my theological applications will be no feather in anyone's cap. I am purposefully trying to avoid theological jargon.

Look past me to what I am trying to say to you. You've got to do your part. You've got to help me keep the spiritual "do-gooders" from carrying a chip on their shoulders and from trying to pick to pieces everything I say.

I bring no hidden agenda to you. I am saying one thing and only one: God showed me a way that has never in the history of the church been used for reclaiming His for Him. Why me? I don't know. All I know is that I have been faithful in getting it to you. Now it's your turn. "Go thou, and do likewise." Did I use that a little out of context? Just making sure you were on your toes.

Now for a fellow who is not a preacher, I got through that pretty well, didn't I? You can tell that I am nervous talking about spiritual things to you and to the men and women of the cloth who are spiritual experts.

Now we are going to get into my arena, where I feel a little more at home. I do several things pretty well and several things pretty average. But I am better at networking and teaching networking than at anything else I do.

Come on. Let's get on over to my turf. The coffee shop is my domain. I am going to take you on an adventure that in your wildest days in graduate school, at seminary, or at the convent, even in your youth, you would never have imagined.

We're going to plow a new field. Never been plowed before. Never been heard of before. Just you and me. For Him.

There are not many worthwhile things that have never been tried in the church. Here's one. It's never been done, except in our pilot projects. This is the day for Team Seven:

> There is one thing stronger than all the armies in the world, and that is an idea whose time has come.
>
> —Victor Hugo

God reveals His will to us from many different sources. You can't listen to every wind that blows, but you'd better listen to some of them. Hannah Whitall Smith said:

> There are four ways in which he reveals his will to us,— through the Scriptures, through providential circumstances, through the convictions of our own higher judgment, and through the inward impressions of the Holy Spirit on our minds. Where these four harmonize, it is safe to say that God speaks.[2]

I was talking with the Catholic bishop of Dallas about the concept, and we had a great visit. He said, "Young Man, Gamaliel, the Apostle Paul's teacher, said, 'If it's of man, it won't last. If it's of God, no man can stop it.'"

You and I are going to make history. We'll be the first kids on the block with the Team Seven concept. Remember:

All roads once weren't.

II. You'll Feel Like the Man Who
First Discovered Fire

Do not follow where the path may lead.
Go instead where there is no path and leave a trail.

—Unknown

The minister was about to deliver his sermon when he remembered an important announcement he had forgotten to make. So he said, "Before I preach, I want to say something."

Because you and I are going to be so engrossed very quickly in the Team Seven concept, I want to "say something" to you first.

Networking the Kingdom is a book on how to network the kingdom through reclamation. Its tool is Team Seven. Team Seven is a new way of attaining church growth. It is a technique to be learned, not a program to be adopted.

Networking the Kingdom has one mission: reclamation. Reclamation of those who once were part of the kingdom fellowship, but now, for whatever reason, aren't.

Networking the Kingdom sounds the reclamation theme on every page just like a leitmotif in a Wagnerian opera. We have ruled out all other subjects for emphasis. Does that mean we are not interested in evangelism or other areas? The answer is simply that there is a great deal of information already written in other areas. If anything, we are over-trained in other areas. We're not trained in this one yet. We're trying to focus on the one subject long enough for God's magnifying glass to get a fire going. He can, if we can get those we are trying to reclaim to hold still long enough, at the Coffee Shop Meeting.

Networking the Kingdom is not particularly a church book. It is a book for church people, based on business principles. Its mission is to reclaim a harvest. Its premise is that the church has done a superior job at teaching, evangelizing, and ministering to its people, and has even known a Great Awakening. But in the process, a lot of "dead bodies" have been left strewn around. They don't seem to fit in anywhere except as fodder for a revival sermon, or as the butt of some unkind person's remark about backslidden hypocrites.

The goal of *Networking the Kingdom* is to marshal those "outside the door" into an army of kingdom recruiters. Hoped-for result: the Great Reclamation.

Networking the Kingdom's marching orders for reclamation are from Jesus, who said:

> If a man has 100 sheep, but 1 of the sheep gets lost, he will leave the other 99 sheep on the hill. He will go to look for the lost sheep.
>
> And if he finds it, he is happier about that 1 sheep than about the 99 that were never lost.
>
> —Matthew 18:12–13

There are many stories in the Bible on reclamation. It seems that the Lord of the Harvest expects to reap where He has sown, and on land He owns. But it also appears that He expects us to be His hands and feet. There is an important parable told by Jesus in Matthew 21:33–43 about a man who leased his vineyard to some farmers and left the country. The farmers refused to give him his part of the harvest and even killed his son. The story has a lot of good lessons. But since you and I are talking about reclamation, as you reread this passage I want you to notice the extent to which He went to reclaim the harvest for the kingdom and His conclusion about those who didn't fulfill the terms of the lease. You know the story so I've only included the beginning and the ending:

> There was a man who owned a vineyard. He put a wall around the vineyard and dug a hole for a winepress. Then he built a tower. He leased the land to some farmers and left for a trip. . . .

> So I tell you that the kingdom of God will be taken away from you. It will be given to people who do the things God wants in his kingdom.
>
> —Matthew 21:33, 43

As I went about my business ventures in networking, I noticed how many casualties there were—those who just didn't make it for some reason or another. Then I would go to church and notice the same thing. One exception. We in the business world seemed to make a more concerted effort at reclaiming our inactive associates than we at the church did. I include myself, too. I am talking about a need, not making a criticism. It was as though we were ashamed to admit that they used to belong to us.

As you read the next few chapters you will come to see how the Team Seven concept was born, and how it evolved to this point. My next question was, "Would anyone else see it?"

Then I wondered how I could discuss the concept with leaders and keep it from leaking out to someone who might take a portion of it, before getting the whole story.

The simpleton will be like a person who reads the rules of chess, plays the first game, and loses. His response: "Chess doesn't work. I tried that, and it just doesn't work."

As surely as "what goes up, must come down," studying the Team Seven concept will call for a response. Momentarily, you may feel that your equilibrium has been shaken. *Networking the Kingdom* is not a devotional book that gives you a warm, fuzzy feeling. Once read, it will call forth action, either to implement its concepts or to dig your heels into the ground. Most will say, "Let's try it. What have we got to lose?"

Most will be right.

But Team Seven, if implemented, will demand performance, results, and skills never before required of church members. Maybe in the business world, but not at church.

It is like the difference between teaching an English class

and coaching a football team. Both teachers may be equally qualified, but the coach loses his job if the team doesn't produce results. The team may have been well coached and may have played well, but he didn't produce the results. The English teacher and the coach both did a good job. But the English teacher was not fired because the work was not placed on display and judged at Saturday afternoon's game.

Team Seven cannot survive without results because your people will quit when they don't get them. At first they will blame themselves, then they will blame anything that moves.

It is important to acknowledge the 80–20 rule of life. Just as in the business world, we at the church can usually get only twenty percent of our church members to tithe, sing in the choir, attend regularly, or teach Sunday School. Team Seven comes under that law, just as it comes under the law of gravity.

There are virtually only two reasons a person will fail with the concepts: Either (1) he or she is unteachable, or (2) he or she cannot handle it emotionally.

Like a child talking with the school counselor, he blames his parents and his background for his plight, for there is only one other place to put the blame. (I believe the current expression is, "I have bad 'tapes' from my childhood.")

If you decide God is in it, and you make a commitment to do it, and you say, "Either I'll get it done, or when you come back, you'll find me standing in a puddle of blood," you'll get it done. You see, we know Team Seven works. We just don't know *who* will work.

Don't be afraid just because it's new. Remember, people have had right and left shoes for only a little over a century. Can you imagine that it took that long before someone asked, "What if we made shoes for the right and left feet?"

As you work through the concept, and begin to realize what Team Seven can do through you for the kingdom, you may begin to feel a little like the man must have felt who first discovered fire. I know I did.

1

My Experience in Networking

Do you see a man skilled in his work?
That man will work for kings.
He won't have to work for ordinary people.
—Proverbs 22:29

Jewell was driving, on our motor-home trip in Yellowstone. "It's right around the curve. You just wait, you think you saw something back there," he said. Earlene was glad we weren't going to eat in the camper today, and that grizzly bear yesterday had discouraged Gladys from ever eating outside again.

It was the last day, and we all had cabin fever. We'd used up all our clean clothes, and we'd finished all the leftovers, exactly as Earlene had planned. Ralph hadn't been able to get into the cupboard and was saying, "Boys, it's past my eating time back at the school."

We had just toured the geyser and mud pot basins of Yellowstone. My creative juices were in overdrive. I was in the early stages of formulating the ideas for the application

1

of the Team Seven concept to the church, which were to
later become *Networking the Kingdom.* My family was helping me give personality names to the geysers and mud pots.
    "There it is!" Jewell yelled and . . .
    I'm getting a little ahead of myself. Let me go back and
catch you up. I won't take long though, because Ralph and I
have to catch a plane.

How I Got into Networking

Let me take you back to Texas to catch you up. For seven
years now, I have been networking full-time for a thirty-
year-old company. The name of it is significant to me but
not to you. It is the concept I am promoting here and not a
company.
    Networking has come of age. It is now taught at the Har-
vard University School of Business. John Naisbitt, in his
book *Megatrends,* discusses the influence of networking
now and in the future. In his wildest thoughts, he probably
never imagined using it in the church. His is a "must-read"
book.
    Usually when the subject of networking comes up, we
think of network marketing companies, both good and bad,
who market their products from friend to friend. These
companies and others use a distributor's natural, and sometimes unnatural, influence to recruit their associates. Obviously, some recruits have abused the concept, but some have
built empires on sound business principles and friendship
relationships.
    I daresay that if you decide to use the concepts taught in
this book, some people will abuse your teachings. In fact,
Jesus didn't get one hundred percent cooperation. He
started with just twelve. *You* can get by with three. Can you
find three in your church who will go with you to the wall?
That's all you need to get started, and we won't need two of
them for about a month.
    If you are unfamiliar with networking, skip this para-
graph. [If you are familiar with the concept, let me make a

couple of observations with you. In network marketing, some choose to sponsor wide first; some prefer to sponsor in depth first. The deciding factor seems to be that if you need or prefer profitability first, you sponsor in width first. If you prefer stability over early profitability, you sponsor in depth first. Some, but not many, can do both simultaneously. I believe that even those who continue to prefer traditional networking in their businesses will readily see the advantages of using the team concept in the church, where profitability is not a factor.]

The following is a capsule definition of what I mean by the term *networking, using the Team Seven concept*:

NETWORKING; USING TEAM SEVEN: Church members reaching their unchurched friends, who in turn reach their friends, who in turn reach their friends until the team is seven friends deep. This means seven new layers of networks for the kingdom. The process goes to infinity because each of the seven, individually and as a team, is working to get a team of seven under himself.

The concepts that I am presenting here are just as applicable to a secular network as to a church and vice versa. The only differences are the product and the message.

Now let me tell you how I was introduced to the networking business. I had purchased an Air Force base, and was recycling the barracks buildings, once used for officers' quarters.

My original plan was to cut the buildings vertically into three sections, and move them as two-story units. The wire bill made that prohibitive, because the buildings would not go under the wires that cross the streets. I remembered the words of George Bernard Shaw:

Some men see things as they are and say "Why?"
I dream things that never were, and say "Why not?"

My problem: The buildings were too tall and the wires were too low.

Solution: "What if? What if we dismantled most of the bottom floor of the unit, ran steel beams under it, jacked it up for a few minutes while the crew quickly dismantled the rest of the bottom floor before that West Texas wind blew it off the beams, let it down, and rolled it out as a one-story unit?"

How important that question: "What if?" It gives you a new perspective. We did it. Pictures of the operation and a story were in some of the big town newspapers. I received a call from a man who had seen the article, and he said, "I have a deal I want to talk with you about."

He was quite successful in real estate, architecture, and banking. We did the real estate deal. One day someone told me he had another business, on the side, that had nothing to do with real estate. So I asked him to tell me about his other business. Three months later he did.

That's a cameo of how I was introduced to networking by my sponsor. He and his wife recruited and trained me.

Team Sponsoring:
The Parent of Team Seven

After a short introduction to the business, I began having at least modest success. In fact, for a fellow who is a teacher and only an average salesman, I felt I was doing great.

But I soon learned that there were three serious problems with network marketing:

1. I couldn't get the people at the ends of the lines of sponsorship to market their products.
2. People quit faster than I could sponsor them.
3. But the killer problem was that I had made competitors of my friends.

Because my sponsors were inactive, I was off in a small town building my business without much outside influence. I thought I was the only one having these problems. But as I began going to seminars and reading books, I soon learned that not only were these common to every distributor in my company, but also of every networking company. They were all having trouble with getting people to market products, with retention of people, and with competition among friends.

How these problems were resolved and how the concept developed are discussed in detail in my book *Team Sponsoring* published by Fleming H. Revell Company. So I won't give you those details here. If you have further interest, you can read that at your leisure. I've already plowed that field.

A Little Speech Became a Big Speech

I never intended to write a book, at least on this subject. But a funny thing happened one day. Actually, it was one evening. It changed my life forever and thrust me onto the world stage as a celebrity without portfolio.

I hadn't intended to do this, but I think I'll just share it with you. Let me set the stage for you. I'm a good storyteller.

I had been networking for about a year from a small town in Texas. I had found a way to solve the three big killer problems for me and my organization. We were having explosive growth. People were marketing; they weren't quitting, and we had them on a team, instead of in competition with each other.

I was starting a new group in Dallas. So I flew down there to work with my small, new group. My upline sponsors heard that I was there, and asked me to bring my small group over to a cafeteria to meet with their group of about fifty people. After I arrived, they asked me if I would talk to the group about my business. It was and is a practice used in networking groups.

I jumped in and told them how we were solving the age-old problems of marketing, retention, and competition through Team Sponsoring and the Seven Deep concept.

Someone recorded it; it came out on tape of the week, and I was thrust onto the world stage.

All of a sudden, I began receiving phone calls from all over the United States from some very important people. Many of these people had multi-million dollar businesses. I received so many calls that I had to get an answering machine. When I would come home from marketing and recruiting, the answering machine would be completely full.

You cannot believe the calls. They would offer to send their private jets if I would come and talk with their groups. Some of the leaders of some of the largest organizations in the world of network marketing flew to my small town to see my operation. When I went to speak for their groups, they picked me up in their private limousines. I had never ridden in a Rolls Royce before.

The world of network marketers beat a path to my doorstep. People would call and say, "We're bringing a busload of people to observe your meetings." That scared me, so I wouldn't tell them where my meetings were. All of a sudden, I was asked to speak before thousands of people each week. They even whisked me off to California, where they did a video of my concepts. I then got even more phone calls.

It is probably obvious to you, as it was to me from the beginning, that all this attention wasn't building my own personal networking business. So I decided to write my concepts down and share them with everyone. The result was *Team Sponsoring: A Practical Guide to Network Marketing.*

I still receive calls almost daily, and I still do some speaking engagements. But at last, I was able to get back to concentrating on my own business.

I am told that the concept is used in every free market in the world where there is network marketing. *Team Sponsoring* is now published in French and is being translated into other languages. Sometimes translators have a difficult time with some of my Tennessee, hillbilly expressions.

If you decide to use the concepts I am sharing with you in this book, you will probably hear some of the typical comments that I receive from time to time.

It is a real joy to be speaking somewhere, and have someone whom I have never met come up and say something like,

"Thanks to you and *Team Sponsoring,* I am at such and such a level in my business." I just smile and say, "Tell me more." Well, what would you say?

The comments are not always positive, though. Sometimes someone will come up and say, "I don't think *Team Sponsoring* will work." Sometimes they say, "I tried that and it didn't work."

As kindly as I can say it, I often respond very softly, "What you had before *Team Sponsoring* came along was traditional networking. If traditional networking is working so well for you, why don't you keep doing that? *Team Sponsoring* is offered as an alternative to those who couldn't make traditional networking work as well as they wanted it to." You see, I don't make any money whether they do well or not. I simply share my ideas.

If you decide to put these concepts to work in your organization or church, you need to be prepared for both responses, also.

Well, that's a little bit about how the concept developed in the business world.

God Gave It to Me

His boundless love supports and contains us as a mighty ocean contains and supports the tiny drops of every wave. With a surging fullness He is forever moving toward us, seeking to fill the creeks and bays of our lives with unlimited resources.
—Martin Luther King, *The Strength To Love*

The most often asked question is, "How did you think up the concept?" Other than what I have told you here and in *Team Sponsoring,* I think of what a seminary professor said when I told him I would not stop until I had earned my doctorate.

He said, "God has a strange way of using a trained mind." I think he was quoting Louis Pasteur.

Long before I had any thought of using the concept in the

church, I said in *Team Sponsoring,* "God gave it to me."
One of my favorite quotes is by Abraham Lincoln, "I'll prepare myself and perhaps my chance will come." Perhaps
this is my chance.

But you know what? All the time that the concept was
raging like wildfire through network organizations everywhere in the world, there was welling up in me an urging
that this should be usable some way in the church. It is so
strong now that I cannot remember when it was not there.
But I remember every detail, hour, and speaker who pulled
it from the deep resources of my being.

2
How Team Seven Evolved for Use in the Church

If one advances confidently in the direction of his dreams, and endeavors to live the life which he has imagined, he will meet with a success unexpected in common hours.
—Henry David Thoreau

I know that it would be more profound if I told you that a bolt of lightning hit me on the head, and I was struck blind like Paul, and there Team Seven was, full grown, ready to be implemented in your organization or church.

The way that it happened was through rather ordinary circumstances. It occurred because people were going about their ordinary tasks of "being found faithful" in small things. You see, we never know when God is going to work His work, do we?

We would all rather be in the limelight, listening to the applause of the crowd. Although He often speaks there, sometimes He speaks to us at the workbench. Evelyn Underhill explains it as well as I have ever heard it explained:

Our place is not the auditorium but the stage—or, as the case may be, the field, workshop, study, laboratory—because we ourselves form part of the creative apparatus of God, or at least are meant to form part of the creative apparatus of God. He made us in order to use us, and use us in the most profitable way; for his purpose, not ours. To live a spiritual life means subordinating all other interests to that single fact. Sometimes our position seems to be that of tools; taken up when wanted, used in ways which we had not expected for an object on which our opinion is not asked, and then laid down. Sometimes we are the currency used in some great operation, of which the purpose is not revealed to us. Sometimes we are servants, left year in, year out to the same monotonous job. Sometimes we are conscious fellow-workers with the Perfect, striving to bring the Kingdom in. But whatever our particular place or job may be, it means the austere conditions of the workshop, not the free-lance activities of the messy but well-meaning amateur; clocking in at the right time and tending the machine in the right way. Sometimes, perhaps, carrying on for years with a machine we do not very well understand and do not enjoy; because it needs doing, and no one else is available. Or accepting the situation quite quietly, when a job we felt that we were managing excellently is taken away. Taking responsibility if we are called to it, or just bringing the workers their dinner, cleaning and sharpening the tools. All self-willed choices and obstinacy drained out of what we thought to be our work; so that it becomes more and more God's work in us.[1]

"What If?"

What frightens me is this. What if the student hadn't called and said God was dealing with him? What if the Bible teacher had not showed up that Sunday? What if the commentator hadn't come that Sunday?

What if the Christian businessman had not been selected for that outstanding award for patriotism and had not been asked to give his testimony at church that Sunday? What if that college campus leader had not told his story on Sunday evening? What if that church had been the kind that shoots its wounded, and had not had a class for singles?

Scary, isn't it? Oh well, I guess it's not too scary to you because I am getting ahead of myself again. I'm sort of getting my boots on before my socks. Let's do some more catching up.

Saturday Night

Let me unfold it for you. It was sort of like a baby being born. You are the first one to whom I've told the whole story.

On Saturday night, my son, Scott, a sophomore at the time at Baylor University in Waco, Texas, called. He is a business major but was serving as an intern youth director at a church in Waco.

This is a paraphrase of what he said. "Dad, I'm loving my work here at the church and especially the music. I don't know if God wants me to be a businessman or a minister of some kind. But if He wants me to work in the church, I want to do something besides just stand up and deliver a sermon or lecture. I feel that very strongly, but I don't know what it is."

We talked and I told him of some creative things that were going on at my church in Dallas. I told him of our singles class, where the teacher gives the lesson, and then a commentator, à la John Chancellor, does a commentary on the lesson. I said, "Wouldn't it be great to have a minister delivering the sermon, and someone standing beside him doing a running commentary? Not comical, but actually doing it. Sort of a man from the congregation doing a response? What if?"

That's a good question when you are trying to get to the bottom of things. "What if?" My boys have used that a lot on me. They'd say, "Dad, what if?"

Scott and I talked about a lot of comical things that could happen there, as well as a lot of meaningful things. I'd still like to try that sometime, if I could find a minister who wanted to try it.

As we talked, I don't remember how it came up, but Scott said, "Dad, wouldn't it be great if we could use your Team concept some way in the church?" We both said "Yes!" and that really brought the laughs. But then we got serious and agreed to seek a way to implement it in the church. I told him I had been thinking about it, but hadn't found a way to use it there. That was one big phone bill. We talked until about 2 A.M.

"Before you hang up, Dad, I want to read you something I read during my prayer time last night." He read:

If the Church really sees itself as the people of God, it is obvious that it can never be a static and suprahistorical phenomenon, which exists undisturbed by earthly space and historical time. The Church is always and everywhere a living people, gathered together from the peoples of this world and journeying through the midst of time. The Church is essentially en route, on a journey, a pilgrimage.

As he read the next line, it jumped out at me as if giving reassurance to introducing a new concept to the church. See if you don't agree.

A church which pitches its tents without looking out constantly for new horizons, which does not continually strike camp, is being untrue to its calling.[2]

Wow!

Sunday Morning

The next morning I walked into Bible Study and sat down as usual. But as the teacher and commentator were doing their thing, my mind was doing wild creative gyrations. "What if this?" and "What if that?"

Then I went to big church. W. Clement Stone and a very prominent businesswoman were being recognized for being outstanding patriots. W. Clement Stone gave a ten-minute talk.

You probably know that he is the president of Combined Insurance Co. of America. Everything he said was brilliant, but one thing he said sent my mind a-whirring. Basically, it was that if the church could ever bring itself to adopt some of the principles that have made so many businesses great, it could have explosive growth.

During the sermon that morning, the pastor stated that he would love to see the church double in the next five years. I was thinking, "I know a way that it can be seven times the size it is in two years." I couldn't wait until church was over.

After Church

After church, I waited until most of the people had finished shaking hands with the pastor. Boy, I couldn't wait for those people to get on through the line. Have you ever noticed that a lot of people want to give a seminar while they are in a receiving line?

I looked him right square in the eye and said, "Were you serious when you said you were interested in seeing the church double in five years?" I don't think too many of the people in the line in front of me had asked him that question. My first cue was the way he looked at me when I asked him that.

I then said, "How would you like to have the church grow to seven times the size it is in two years?" He knew me well enough to know I wasn't kidding. I said, "Remember that book that my publisher sent you that I wrote called *Team Sponsoring*? I am about to reconcile, in my mind, a way to use the concept in the church. As it becomes clearer, I will let you know."

He said, "Great. Keep me posted."

Sunday Night

You won't believe what happened that same Sunday evening in the service. The guest speaker was Bill Bright from Campus Crusade.

Mr. Bright told how he had thought of going into mass evangelism. But he decided on a ministry of one to one. He told of his "sons" in the ministry and even great-grandsons. The theme of his message was that the church must somehow get better at discipling the "ones" instead of concentrating so much on the masses. He said it much more eloquently, but this was the thrust of his message, as I understood it.

Man, my creative juices went to flowing again. I had another piece of the puzzle. After church I told the pastor that it was becoming clearer how we were going to get the church doubled ahead of his schedule. He grinned in agreement, but that was the extent of the conversation.

After Church Sunday Night

Scott and I talked again that night about the day's revelations and insights. I didn't have to explain to him the *Team Sponsoring* concept, since he was already at the first major level in our networking business. By now the ideas were coming out like machine-gun fire, and we couldn't get them down fast enough.

The Following Week

The following week it simmered, jelled, and began to take a form of its own. The following Sunday I told the pastor that I now had it close enough that I could present it to his staff one on one. After swearing them all to secrecy, I gave them the basic thrust. Each in his or her turn responded with awe.

A Couple of Weeks Later

About two weeks later I presented it to the pastor and my close friend, the education director. We had another meeting about a week later to explain it in further detail to the pastor and another of his associates. The pastor's basic response was, "It's the most profound concept I've ever seen introduced to the church. Let's do it."

Tragedy Strikes

We decided to begin. Before we got very far into it, tragedy struck our church. *The Dallas Morning News* carried a sad, tragic, and heartwrenching story. We all died a thousand deaths and wept for this loss in the kingdom.

In its life and death struggle, the church closed ranks with intent on survival, and Team Seven was lost in the shuffle.

I kept remembering the song, "He Maketh No Mistake," but the words were getting fainter and fainter.

A Casual Lunch Became a Significant Lunch

About six months later, one evening one of my distributors invited me to go with him to a luncheon for Christian business men and women. I had been once before. After the lunch, he introduced me to the pastor whose church was sponsoring the lunch. They were already doing first-level networking. The history of the church has been first-level networking. That means the church members contact the prospects they know.

A few days later, I received a call from the pastor's secretary, asking me if I would have lunch with the pastor. We set the date. Neither of us knew of the other's interest in networking.

I had been writing a little every day on *Networking the Kingdom,* and was pretty well through with it, but I was waiting for our church to get a new preacher. Like with Moses and the Promised Land, God didn't want to wait, evidently. So we went on.

My new pastor friend from the business luncheon said, "At a big church that has everything, you'll never know if it was the Lord or the location. If you do it at our church, and it works, you'll know it was God." Made sense to me.

Now if you were writing a story, how would you make Team Seven turn all the corners it turned? John McKay, who used to be the soloist with the James Robison Crusade, also used to sing in my church choir. One Sunday he sang this song for us, and it has haunted me ever since. What do you think?

> My Father's way may twist and turn,
> My heart may throb and ache,
> But in my soul, I'm glad I know,
> He maketh no mistake.
> —A. M. Overton

3

What Is Networking?

eam Sponsoring will give you detailed information on networking and how to do it. If you decide to become a student of networking, you will want to master its concepts. Without rewriting the book, here is a little information you will need.

In the business world, networking is where I recommend a business to you, you recommend it to a friend, and he recommends it on to another friend, and so forth. At some point, when an associate has enough business volume in his organization, he breaks away and deals directly with the company. That is what keeps it from becoming a pyramid. The person who sponsored the one who broke away receives an override from that person's business. Not all companies do this, but the better ones do.

Here are some terms and expressions you will need to know, so you don't get lost in networking jargon:

Networking Terms and Expressions

NETWORKING; USING TEAM SEVEN: Church members reaching their unchurched friends, who in turn reach their friends, who in turn reach their friends until the team is seven friends deep. This means seven new layers of networks for the kingdom. The process goes to infinity because each of the seven, individually and as a team, is working to get a team of seven under himself.

SPONSOR: You recommend a company, concept, or church to a friend. If the friend joins, you become the sponsor.

UPLINE: Those sponsored above you.

DOWNLINE: Those sponsored below you.

TEAM: Those associates you have introduced to the network. You are also a part of the person's team who introduced you to the network.

LEG: Same as team.

BREAK AWAY: When an associate in a business organization attains so much dollar volume, he breaks away and deals directly with the company. In the church, when a team leader gets seventy-five (a unit) in his organization, he breaks away from his upline sponsor, and deals directly with the pastor and staff.

FIRST-LEVEL NETWORKING: You introduce a friend to the network, and personally sponsor him, rather than placing him on a team in depth. This is often called traditional networking, or working in width. It is still the preferred method of sponsoring by many. Until Team Seven, first-level networking was the only kind of networking the church had ever used on purpose. Sometimes by accident the church went to second-level networking, but seldom on purpose, and almost never went past second-level networking. Jesus was the exception. He worked in depth. (See the Team Seven logo.)

SECOND-LEVEL NETWORKING: You, or one of your team members, places a prospect under someone on your first level. This can go on through layers and layers of networks, on into infinity. This is done as a team and is called working in depth.

NETWORK LAYER: One new person or family that comes into your church or organization. They bring their entire network onto the scene, intentionally or unintentionally.

TEAM LEADER: One who has recruited, or helped to recruit, seven new church members, seven deep under himself or herself.

TEAM MEMBER: A church member, individual or family, in the process of becoming a team leader.

UNIT: 75 people. A team leader has a unit when he has three teams seven deep, with each having three teams seven deep.

THE TEN STEPS TO NETWORKING THE KINGDOM: The rudiments of networking.

FOLLOW-UP PACK: A packet of materials containing a church bulletin, a tape from the pastor of the church, and a couple of other pieces of literature, no more than three. The "follow-up pack" is given to a prospect after you have met with him or her at a Coffee Shop Meeting. (Consult the Appendix.)

FIRST SIX TAPES: These six tapes teach you how to make an effective "Approach," how to do a Coffee Shop Meeting, how to make a list, how to pull names from your team members and prospects, and how to keep your team members going. (Consult the Appendix for ordering instructions.)

AUTOMATIC SHIPMENT: Automatic Shipment of a tape each month, for the purpose of getting current and correct information through the organization. (Consult the Appendix.)

VIDEO: A presentation of *Networking the Kingdom,* and a full explanation of how to implement the Team

Seven technique in your organization. (Consult the
Appendix.)

That's an oversimplification of networking and of some of
the terms and tools we will be talking about as we go along.
The information is designed to give you hope, not confidence. What I just gave here is only a peek at networking
and is sort of like looking at the Grand Canyon at night with
a flashlight. So don't quit here.

Monkey See; Monkey Do

If you decide to use this in your church or organization, your
organization will eventually become so large that you can no
longer communicate individually with each. Yet you want
them all to have the same information. How do you do that?
That's the purpose of having everyone read *Networking the
Kingdom* and listen to their first six tapes. That way, they all
get the basics of what they need. You must insist that those
who participate obtain at least that amount of information.
Then Automatic Shipment of a tape each month keeps them
current.

I tell my team members, "If I were a doctor, and I gave
you advice which you did not heed, I don't think I would
want the responsibility for you. I might ask you to get another doctor." We can't be that strong at the church, because
we all have the same Great Physician. My point is this: They
don't have to do what I recommend, but they do if they want
to succeed.

When I recruit a team member, I schedule another meeting with him then and there. It's the Tupperware principle.
The first goal is not to sell something, but to schedule another meeting. I tell my new recruit, "I expect you to have
read the book and listened to your first six tapes when we
get back together."

He doesn't have to do it. But he will never do it, if I am
not strong. I am not talking about being bossy. I am talking
about helping someone build an organization.

Networking the Kingdom and the six tapes give your team members the basics of what we are doing, so you don't have to spoon-feed them. You understand that you must do things and teach things that can be duplicated. "Read the book and listen to your six tapes, and teach that to your team members," is duplicatable through any size organization. It is easily understood. Monkey see; monkey do.

If they don't know the ABCs, how can I teach them to write? If they don't know the multiplication tables, how can I teach them math? The book and the six tapes teach them the ABCs and the multiplication tables, so to speak.

I am teaching you things that can be duplicated. If your kingdom network grows to ten thousand in your downline, and some will, you must have a way of dispersing the rudiments of your teachings in a condensed and concise form.

Even if you have a little bitty group or church, you are only a year or so away from having a gigantic network if you master the principles I am teaching you here.

No one has to do anything complicated. But everyone has to learn to do very well, the same, simple things over and over, or the process breaks down. You know the story. You are ahead of me. But it illustrates the point.

The boss gave this new fellow a five-gallon bucket of paint and a brush, and said, "Paint that yellow line down that highway."

At closing time, the boss said, "How far did you paint?"

The new man said, "Five miles."

"Excellent," said the boss. "Do that again tomorrow."

At closing, "How far did you paint?"

"Two miles," said the new man.

The boss said, "Hmmm."

At closing on the third day, he said to the boss, "I only got a half of a mile."

"That's not too good. I think I had better find someone else to paint that yellow line," said the boss.

The new man said, "But, boss, you don't realize how far I am from the bucket now!"

The further down your line your team members get from

you, the more your teachings are going to get watered down. Tapes, books, and seminars get that information down them in a duplicatable system. More later.

It is not necessary that you read *Team Sponsoring,* but it is recommended. "Why?" It contains techniques to help you further develop and implement your networking-the-kingdom skills.

Disregard the part about company names and products. Go for the concepts. Because I have already covered the subject of network marketing there, I have included here only the briefest comments that are necessary for clarification. About a thimbleful. As I talk with you here, I am assuming that you are a leader in some capacity for your group. It may be that you are the head of a team, the pastor, priest, or other staff member of some organization that is interested in learning this concept for growth of your group.

You may want to read from *Team Sponsoring* at least chapter 6, "Traditional Concepts," and chapter 7, "Contemporary Concepts." The chapters are brief, concise, and in layman's terms. You can already tell I am a pedagogue, can't you?

I don't mean to sound bossy, but I mean to sound strong. You don't have to do any of the things I recommend to you. But you have to do everything exactly as I teach you, if you expect to work the concept successfully. Remember, we are on my turf now.

Joe Church Member: "I Tried Networking One Time."

If for no other reason than to be able to answer the person who says, "I tried networking one time and quit," you may want to thoroughly read *Team Sponsoring.* You can then say, "But you tried the traditional way; let me show you the contemporary way." Better still, let him read the book himself.

I say to the person who says that to me, "I don't care if you don't want to do it, but at least don't do it for the right reason."

Is it beginning to become clear to you why I think you need a basic understanding of network marketing? It is likely that almost every person in your church or parish has a friend or family member who has tried network marketing at one time or another.

I can assure you that not all those experiences were successful. In fact, if the truth were known, had they been successful, they would probably have continued.

Here is the good news. Most of those old experiences came from traditional networking. I tell folks, "I'm at least average and I couldn't make it work either. Let's give the new concept a shot."

Is There a Need to Network the Kingdom?

The sky is not less blue because the blind man does not see it.
—Danish Proverb

What we want, it seems to me, is an implosion and an explosion of growth within the church. I think you will agree with me that the church has grown incestuous in its thinking.

The majority of our leads come from our own members. Most of our thinking comes from within. Rarely are we infused with outside thought. That's probably good for the most part. But how do we break out of the walls of the church to reach the community?

A visitor visits as a guest of a family of the church on Sunday. He drops his visitor's card into the offering plate, or however you do it at your service. His name winds up on the prospect list of the church. Thursday night at visitation, a person whom he has never met draws his name. At 8:00 that evening during the news, this stranger knocks on his door. I'm not criticizing. I'm just saying, that's the best we have.

I've heard it said, and I think you will agree, that in all too many cases the statement is true, "God must have His hand on the church, for how else could you explain the success it has had with the haphazard way it has been run?" This is not true of all churches, of course, but too many.

Church Capacity 1600;
Church Attendance 300

One of the first things that one pastor said to me when we first discussed networking the kingdom was, "There are churches all over the world that are just like ours. Here we are in a dying part of downtown, with a church building that holds sixteen hundred, and with three hundred in attendance."

I looked around at the pictures of him preaching in front of thousands of people when he was the director of youth for a great denomination in Texas.

I asked myself, "What's wrong?" Here was a dynamic, handsome, young, energetic minister willing to sweat blood for the church. I met some of the people. They had the same desires he did. I knew what God's desires were. What was missing?

He and the leaders were doing everything they had been taught and trained to do. They were taking their cues from the fastest-growing churches in the country.

What Was Missing?

People! They were doing everything they were supposed to do to, with, or for the people. It's just that all those people had already had it done to, with, or for them.

They did not have an effective recruiting mechanism for infusing new blood into the organization. Oh, they had the traditional things. But those were hackneyed by now.

By his sheer personality, charisma, spiritual warmth, and integrity, the pastor was able to attract an occasional sharp couple to visit the church. When they saw no other attractive or unattractive couples their age joining, they politely slipped away. Now I can sugarcoat this, or I can tell it like it is. I hope you are tracking with me. I don't mean to offend anyone. If your church is growing and vibrant, you don't need this. "They that are whole need not a physician, but they that are sick."

Sometimes God just chooses to pour out His blessing in an unusual way on a person's ministry. And sometimes it's just because God put us in an area where we are getting the natural growth of the city. But I have some buddies whom God loves too, who pastor in areas where the city moved. What do you do then? You sure don't strut.

It is easy for us to strut when the new highway comes in front of our church, connecting with the other highway going north and south and we have the corner lot. But it's a horse of a different color when the new highway bypasses our church and the old highway used to go right beside it. Now the sign on the highway says, ""OUR CHURCH, TWO MILES THAT WAY." And some member says, "It doesn't seem like our pastor packs 'em in like he used to."

Solution

If the problem is that we don't have enough new people, then we need a recruiting mechanism. The Team Seven concept has as its biggest weakness and greatest criticism that it recruits people faster than they can be trained.

If you continue to recruit faster than you train, it is the equivalent of outrunning your headlights.

4

Traditional Church Structure of Leads

"Would you tell me, please, which way I ought to go from here?"

"That depends a good deal on where you want to get to," said the Cat.

"I don't much care where—" said Alice.

"Then it doesn't matter which way you go," said the Cat.

—Lewis Carroll, *Alice's Adventures in Wonderland*

When a church member brings a prospect to church, that is using our first-level network. Historically, first-level networking is what the church has done. We're deadly at first-level networking. But for some reason it never dawned upon us to pull a name out of a prospect and then pull a name out of that prospect's prospect.

When a church member's prospect brings a prospect to church that is second-level networking. When a church member's prospect's prospect brings a prospect to church, that is third-level networking. The goal is to find one out of the seven to keep the networking going through multiple new networks. It goes on until kingdom come.

The reason for the number seven is that the odds are that one in seven will emulate what you do. If we can get one team leader out of every seven, the networking goes in depth to infinity. The deeper it goes, the faster it goes.

The hardest part is to get the first seven going. It's like a freight train. It's hard to get it going; it takes a lot of effort. But boy, when it gets to going, don't get in front of it.

In the past, prospects just joined the church. A neighbor invited a neighbor, occasionally on purpose, but usually by accident. That was first-level networking. As a result, as the Cat said to Alice, "it didn't much matter" where they were placed in the structure for future recruiting. We hadn't even thought of structure at that point. We hadn't thought to ask of our new recruits, "Whom do you know?"

Let's talk for a moment about the importance of growing, and then we'll talk about how.

Let's say we are dealing with a church with 250 talents or members as the case may be. The size could be 2500 or 25,000. At the beginning of the year, how many we start with isn't important. It is important that we know how many we have. The reason is that at the end of the year, the Lord of the Harvest may come back to see what we've done with those 250, 2,500, or 25,000 talents. Do you remember the story of the talents in Matthew 25:14–30? You remember that he gave one servant five bags of money (talents), another two and another one. Notice what he said about the servant who hid his one bag of money:

> So the master told his other servants, "Take the bag of money from that servant and give it to the servant who has ten bags of money.
> Everyone who uses what he has will get more. He will have much more than he needs. But the one who does not use what he has will have everything taken away from him."
> —Matthew 25:28–29

As churches, we've sort of "hidden out," when the subject of hiding our talents came up. We've been careful to call the members to task about burying their talents, though. It appears to me that sometimes the Lord might want to look over the church's books at the end of the year. How many talents we start with is not the point. How many we have at the end may be.

We excuse ourselves by saying, "We're not interested in just bringing in a bunch of people. All the staff ever talks about is numbers. God isn't interested in numbers." Oh? The story of the talents shows that He not only appears very interested in numbers, but also in results. In fact, He dealt very severely with the servant that didn't produce any numbers.

It seems to me that God is not only interested in calling the members into accountability, but also the church as a whole. I heard someone say one time, "The church is the only organization on earth that a person can join, never attend, never give a dime to, and at his funeral, have it said, 'He died in good fellowship.'"

Every time there is a presidential election, a favorite question is, "Are you better off or worse off as a result of the incumbent's performance?"

My question is, "Is the church better or worse off since you and I joined it?" Scary question. What kind of a church are we going to leave our children? And their children? Will it be larger, smaller, average, great, spiritual, lukewarm, or what?

If we had to run for election, on the basis of our performance in the kingdom, would they reelect us, or would they throw us, and our whole party, out? What a disturbing thought! I think God must have been thinking about what we as a church were going to leave for our children's inheritance, when He said:

> A good man leaveth an inheritance
> to his children's children.
> —Proverbs 13:22 (King James Version)

How It Usually Happens

As I have said, we have been fantastic at first-level networking. We "tag 'em and target 'em," and they don't usually get away from us. But traditionally, when a member brings a guest to church, it is an accident if it goes past first-level networking. Seldom is an effort made in the way of getting a lead from that new person.

Now understand that I am only talking about the fact that we have stayed in first-level networking. I am not criticizing the technique we used. I'm just pointing it out in order to later make the point of the significance of networking in depth and the Coffee Shop Meeting. We never knew to go past our prospects into their network. Here is the best that we could expect to happen. One of these two things:

(1) The visitor, Sam, the salesman, may or may not put his name on a visitor's card and drop it in the offering plate. If he does this (and he may not), his name is typed on a visitation card. These cards are shuffled and dealt to the person in his age group. (2) Or this occurs. The member introduces the visitor, Sam, the salesman, to the pastor and says, "Why don't you two get together for lunch some-time?" That's called the "Woo 'em and dump 'em on the pastor" technique.

Just today I visited a medium-sized growing church, and the minister said from the pulpit, as he welcomed the visitors, "If you have ever filled out a visitor's card, you know I've tried to catch you. You've got to forgive me if I haven't gotten to you. Keep your house clean 'cause I'm coming."

I'm not criticizing. I'm just acknowledging that that is the system. But the person who criticizes the Coffee Shop Meeting by saying, "I don't want to discuss God's work in a coffee shop," is convinced that the above two techniques are more "holy." What I say is, use both.

If it's all left up to the staff, how many hurting people do you think the pastor can continue to meet with for lunch, or personally visit in their homes, and keep his or her health and sanity? At the most, he or she can have seven lunches a week, because that is all the lunches there are in a week. And doesn't it appear logical that the pastor's spouse might want to be joined for lunch one of those seven days? What do you think?

Once the Person Joins the Church

Now let's suppose that the pastor has had a successful lunch with the prospect, Sam, the salesman, and begins meeting and counseling and bonding with him. The next time we hear of Sam, he is a full-fledged member of the church.

This is how it looks:

> pastor
> Sam

Next month the same thing happens. Same result. Only the name is changed: Nellie, the nurse.

Two months later our chart looks like this:

> pastor
> Nellie   Sam

It's two more months before we get another new one. None of these are coming from the same people. These are all new leads from other members. All first level. Paul, the plumber, joins us.

Looks like this:

> pastor
> Nellie   Sam   Paul

By the sixth month, Bob, the bowling alley man, has joined.

> pastor
> Nellie   Sam   Paul   Bob

In the ninth month we get two more new members, and in the eleventh month we get one more. None in December. We were doing the Christmas pageant. In a moment we'll look at the results from the last year's work by our two hundred and fifty member church. We plan to present these new talents to the Lord on His birthday.

What If We Could Look Through the Eyes of Jesus?

Have you ever wondered how God might go about checking His books? We know He does. He even has a book in the Bible called Numbers. (I don't think that's why he called it that, though.) I got to thinking about this one day. Do you ever wonder about things like that? Let's use our imagination a minute.

"What if?" Let's try that question here, and see where it takes us. "What if? . . ." Do you reckon if, at our church, He decided to look over the books, it might not go something like this?:

We say, "Lord, look at our organizational chart and see our new members."

We hand him the neatly prepared thick file that was prepared by the church's own C.P.A. and say, "Here, Jesus. Just cast your eyes upon this piece of work."

Jesus graciously receives the folder, and gently responds, "Good-looking document. But if it's all right, I'll have someone get our own file; I'm a little more familiar with our record system. Besides that, if I didn't use our copy, it would probably hurt our C.P.A.'s feelings. Like most accountants, he's unusually sensitive about his own figures. But he is, more so, because he used to be a tax man."

Jesus turns and says, "Matthew, would you get me this year's volume of *The Lamb's Book of Life*?"

He reviews it, strokes His chin, and says, "Hum. Let's see now. I gave you 250 talents and you gained 7 talents. While I'm in here, let me look at the chart of another church out in Arizona. Hum. I gave them 2,500 talents. I believe you call them members, and they have 70 new talents. I have another file on another church in. . . . Oh, I'd better not name that town; you'd know that church. Got to keep these things confidential. I gave them 25,000 talents and they picked up 700 new talents.

"Each of you did exactly the same percentages. The church with 25,000 members got the same return on their talents as the church with 250 members. Let me turn over here to the diagram you have drawn. Hum."

Jesus looks over the chart, and this is how it looks as He reviews the books for the year:

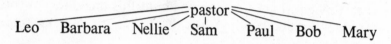

Leo   Barbara   Nellie   Sam   Paul   Bob   Mary

Now if the Chairman of the Board looked at this, these would probably be his observations and questions. Let's imagine that Jesus is Chairman of the Board because He certainly could be if He wanted to. Do you think the conversation might go something like this?

1. Jesus: "How many were contacted by current church members?" We answer, "All of them."

2. "How many were recommended by new members who joined this year?" Answer: "None of them."

3. "How many were asked, 'Whom do you know?'" Answer left blank.

4. "Would you have been less spiritual had you asked, 'Whom do you know?'" Answer: "No, Sir."

5. "Would you have been less spiritual had you contacted one of the new member's prospects?" Answer: "No, Sir."

6. "How many did the pastor or staff have a major time commitment in prior to their joining?" Answer: "All."

7. "Was there any effort made to get the seven new talents or members together as a team in order to harvest their collective networks or abilities?" Answer: "What are you talking about?"

Jesus says, "I have one final question for you."

8. "Can you think of any way that you can better harvest this year's crop?" Answer from the church: "Yes, Sir. We can try harder."

About that time, Joe, the mechanic, jumps up and yells, "Lord, we ought to try networking the kingdom, using Team Seven!"

Then Dave Discontent speaks up and says, "Lord, we don't want to just run a bunch of people through the church. We like the closeness we have. A bunch of people would ruin all our small groups. We know you like to harvest where you didn't plant. We don't want to use our friends to get leads out of them. We can minister better if we know the people who are our own personal leads, rather than those names we get from the new members. We don't want to use people, and we have nothing in common with them."

Jesus looks around at us and says, "Hum. Interesting comments. Keep me posted."

He excuses Himself, and says, "I have to go up and review some more books." As He walks off down the hall, toward the elevator that only has the "up" arrow, He looks in deep thought. He doesn't say it, but do you think He might be thinking, "I've already told them, 'The fields are white unto harvest,' and it looks like the harvest is about to rot on the vine."

The last thing we see is the corner of His white robe that gets caught as the elevator door closes and the corner of the robe slips out of sight.

End of dream?

Lettuce Grows Above the Ground; Carrots Grow Below the Ground

Here is a story I remember from my childhood. Mr. Fox had caught Mr. Rabbit and was about to eat him. Mr. Rabbit said, "If you won't eat me, I'll show you how to have all you want to eat."

"How?" said Mr. Fox.

"Let's go into farming together. I get half, and you get half. One of us will get what grows above the ground and the other will get what grows under the ground. Okay?"

"Great. What shall we plant?"

Mr. Rabbit said, "Do you want your half above the ground or under the ground?"

"I'll take everything that grows below the ground."

"Good choice. Let's plant lettuce."

When they harvested the crop, Mr. Fox was mad because all the good stuff was above the ground, and only the root under the ground.

Mr. Rabbit said, "It was your choice. Why don't you take everything above the ground next year." Mr. Fox agreed.

You're right. That year they planted carrots.

The moral of the story is this. You use the same skills and techniques for farming below the ground as you do above the ground. Whether you plant above the ground or below the ground has to do with the crop you plant. You can harvest either place.

Team Seven is a method of harvesting in depth. You don't stop working in width. Just because you plant carrots, you don't stop planting lettuce.

The Lord of the Harvest is the Lord of depth as well as width. He harvests underground as well as above ground. So does the grim reaper.

Every problem has in it the seeds of its own solution. If you don't have any problems, you don't get any seeds.

—Norman Vincent Peale

5

Team Seven Explained

So the two men went with Jesus. . . . One of the men was
Andrew. . . . The first thing Andrew did was to find his
brother, Simon. . . . The next day Jesus . . . found Philip.
. . . Philip found Nathanael and told him.
—John 1:39–45

Please notice that Jesus, the Master Networker, showed us
how to break into second- and third-level networks. He
already had His team four deep within two days. He did it so
well that it took us two thousand years to realize what He
had done. According to John 1:39–45, this is what it looked
like by the second day:

Jesus
Andrew
Peter
Philip
Nathanael

35

By now it looks something like this:

T E A M

/ Jesus
/ Andrew
/ Peter
/ Philip
/ Nathanael
/ You
/ Me
/ Neighbor

I don't know why it was concealed for two thousand years. Maybe we just needed someone who wasn't a professional, someone who wasn't too close to it, with a new perspective to search out the matter and ask, "What if?"

> It is the glory of God to conceal a thing:
> but the honour of kings is to search out a matter.
> —Proverbs 25:2 (King James Version)

We'll get back to that in a while, but let me begin by telling you that everything that is associated with Team Seven is plugged into your current program. You do not change one thing. It does not cost the church a dime, and it uses the church's greatest asset: its people.

Team Seven starts as a quiet, gentle movement inside the church. It soon reaches into unimagined networks in the community, causing an implosion and explosion of gigantic proportions. It is so easily begun that it is never announced from the pulpit and requires no promotion or puffery.

The Lord of Width Is Also the Lord of Depth

> I am guiding you in wisdom.
> And I am leading you to do what is right.
> —Proverbs 4:11

The Lord of width is also the Lord of depth. Some people will probably argue that with you. But the same people probably argued that the world was flat.

Team Seven is a technique of recruiting in depth for prospects for your church. It is like gravity, or a "B flat" in music; it is neither sacred nor secular.

If someone is sensitive and spiritual now in his witnessing, he will be sensitive and spiritual in his Team Seven witnessing. If he has people skills now, he will have people skills with the Team Seven concept. If he is a backbiter now, he will be a backbiter in his Team Seven work.

Team Seven only brings out more of what a person already is, usually the better part, because he achieves success so much faster.

How to Begin

In Team Seven, we begin with the pastor. You, a church member, desire to become a team leader and build a team of seven new church members. (A team member is described as one person or one family with children.) You of course are already a church member, and are placed directly under the pastor like so:

pastor

you

Our goal is to penetrate seven layers of networks that are not available to the church at this time. (Actually six, since you personally already know number one.)

You know Joe, the mechanic, who used to go to a church somewhere, but has dropped out for one reason or another. You invite Joe, and when he joins the church, he goes on your team as number 1. Your team now looks like this:

pastor

you

mechanic

You now say to the mechanic, "Joe, whom do you know who is not going to church anywhere now?"

Joe introduces you to Don, the dentist. (Notice at this exact point, the church has broken into a network that it never in its wildest dreams could have touched. Sometimes accidentally it did, but seldom on purpose. Team Seven teaches us to do on purpose what we have been doing by accident.)

Same process. You and Joe go talk to the dentist.

pastor

you

mechanic

dentist

You, as the leader, go with Joe to ask Don, the dentist, "Whom do you know, who is not attending church?"

(Please note that we did not call you a team leader at this point, because you do not yet have a team seven deep. Also, don't let Joe go by himself. He is not yet trained. You are. Get him started studying *Networking the Kingdom* and listening to his first six tapes on Team Seven. You are going to go to all these coffees until you have become a team leader and have developed a team leader. At that point, you will have cloned yourself. You will be there when each is born, so to speak. That is a major difference from the usual visitation program. In Team Seven, we do it as a team. The deeper the team goes, the more momentum. Remember the story about the train.)

Don, the dentist, says, "I know a preacher who lost his church. He is a bartender now." (Get Don started on the book and tapes.)

pastor

you

mechanic

dentist

ex-preacher

The ex-preacher says, "I don't know a soul. But I'd like to be involved. Count me in." (Get the ex-preacher started on his training: book and six tapes.)

Pull another name out of one of the others, or you put in another name. (If you cannot get a name out of any of your team members, you put in another name from your own list and keep going. No one can stop you.) The dentist says, "How about Betty, the barmaid?"

pastor
you
mechanic
dentist
ex-preacher
barmaid

The barmaid says, "My uncle owns a bank, and he and his wife aren't attending anywhere." (Get Betty's training started. Have her read *Networking the Kingdom* and listen to her first six tapes.)

pastor
you
mechanic
dentist
ex-preacher
barmaid
banker

The banker says, "We have a new symphony conductor. I'll get him and his wife and children." (Get the banker started on the book and tapes.)

pastor
you
mechanic
dentist
ex-preacher
barmaid
banker
conductor

The conductor says, "The reason I moved to this town is that the rest of my family lives here. I'll bring my brother and his family. He is an attorney for a major hotel chain." (Teach two things first: Read the book and listen to the six tapes. Get the conductor started on the book and six tapes.)

pastor

you

mechanic

dentist

ex-preacher

barmaid

banker

conductor

attorney

Now your team is seven deep, and all seven are already trained. The training is duplicatable. Your best networkers will be those who will do the simple things over and over again. This is all done one on one, or two on one. Two on one is when two team members go to see a prospect. Like Jesus said to do it.

Watch out for the person who wants to reinvent the wheel. People will come to you with all kinds of harebrained ideas to beat the system. Watch out. Someone will come to you with an idea to put an ad in the paper so you can recruit a whole bunch. Seems harmless enough, but watch out.

Remember the story of how many seeds there are in an apple? About five or six seeds, I think. But if you plant the seeds? A tree. Plant the seeds from the tree. An orchard. Plant the seeds from the orchard. A dynasty!

Team Seven isn't complicated. It is simple, but not easy. I don't have an easy method to recommend to you.

Now that we have Team I trained and really humming, we are going to build Team II. Before we start though, let's make a couple of observations.

How many from Team I were already in the church's network? Correct. Only one. The church has now penetrated seven layers of networks. We're just getting started.

Build a Second Team of Seven

Next you build and teach your second team of seven. (You only have two things to remember: recruit and train. Recruit the prospects of your new recruits. Train each by starting them on *Networking the Kingdom* and their first six tapes.)

When you finish Team II, your organization should now look something like this, but not exactly like this. (It doesn't have a mind of its own. It goes where you make it go. Remember, let it become like a Lego set though, and not a model airplane set.)

```
                    pastor
                    you
                      |
   1                mechanic
   2                dentist
   3                ex-preacher
   4                barmaid
   5                banker
   6                conductor
   7                attorney
```

Now build and train Team III. When you finish building and training your Team III, your organization should now look a little like this:

```
                    pastor
                    you
                      |
   1                mechanic         1
   2                dentist          2
   3                ex-preacher      3
   4                barmaid          4
   5                banker           5
   6                conductor        6
   7                attorney         7
```

Clone Yourself in Each Team

Now go back into each team and clone yourself. Remember the chances are that you will only get one in seven to do what you did.

Your teams when finished should look something like this:

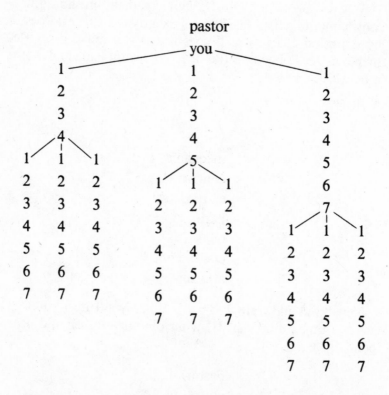

Wow! Look at all the new networks! In your wildest imagination, could you have put those names together?

You never know which one it is who will be used to duplicate your effort. So you train them all. They won't all take training. But if you are ever going to break the twenty-four-hour time barrier, this is how you break it. You must disciple that person, and teach him everything that you have been taught.

The leaders will come to the top. But you must train all of your team. If you are like I am, and I am at least average, you will practically always pick out the wrong one. You can't tell who will become the team leader, so you train them all. You just don't know how God is working, or what is going on inside a person's bosom.

Anybody that says he does, will probably also tell you he knows the hour and minute of the Second Coming. Watch out for him.

When Do the Teams Break Away from Their Team Leader?

Just for a moment, let's review the definition of the term *break away* and then we'll discuss its implications for networking the kingdom:

BREAK AWAY: When an associate in a business organization attains so much dollar volume, he breaks away and deals directly with the company. In the church, when a team leader gets seventy-five, a unit, in his organization, he breaks away from his upline team leader and deals directly with the pastor and staff.

You can see that anyone down in any of the teams can start a team of seven and become a "you" all over again. Every person becomes his own C.E.O. for his team. Who is above you in your line of sponsorship is not nearly as important as who is under you. The power of this is that it goes to infinity.

But when does a person break away from you and deal directly with the pastor and church? In most networks, there is a breakaway point. In marketing, that is what keeps it from becoming a pyramid. By breaking away, it becomes multi-level.

Since the church is not marketing a product, there is no need for breaking away from a legal standpoint. But there is a potential danger that is scary, and reasonably so, to most pastors. The danger is the concentration of that much potential power in someone other than the pastor.

A new team leader and his group break away from his old team leader and deal directly with the church staff. This happens after the new group becomes a unit. This is done in order to keep an unscrupulous member from becoming a power broker. Also, groups this size are more easily managed.

That would ordinarily be when the new team leader has built three teams of seven, and then helped one person under each of those three teams build three teams of seven each. See the above example. You will notice that there are about twenty-five on each team ($3 \times 7 = 21$ plus a few extra), so the three teams together have about seventy-five ($3 \times 25 = 75$). That is what we call a unit.

The same should happen when the new team leader has a newer team leader under him or her who has built three teams of seven with three teams of seven under him or her. To put it simply, every time there are seventy-five in a new group (a unit), that unit, with its team leader, breaks away from the previous team leader, and begins to deal directly with the church staff.

But they always remain in the old team leader's group, too. It's like when a daughter becomes a mother, she is still a daughter. But she moves out and sets up housekeeping elsewhere, and only goes over to her mother's house to visit.

Breaking away also means that the church and staff take over the guidance of the new team leader. The new team leader continues to lead, nurture, and bond with his organization. He also still maintains a bond with his old team leader.

The old team leader is now free from the details of teaching everything to him. The staff takes over here. He has now weaned the new team leader and cloned himself. The old team leader now has the time to go out and build another unit.

6
Depth Is Good; Width Is Good

I love y'all. I'm not abandoning my country and western fans; I'm just adding another layer of fans.

—Dolly Parton

I heard Dolly Parton being interviewed on TV when she first started singing contemporary-pop music. Her country and western fans were up in arms. They thought she was abandoning them. She was doing a little damage control. She told them she wasn't quitting doing any of the things she was already doing. She said in the interview, "I'm not abandoning my country and western fans; I'm simply adding another layer of fans."

Let's review for a moment. When we invite a friend to church, that's first-level networking.

When we invite that person's friend to church, that's networking in depth, or second-level networking. When we invite to church that person's friend's friend, that's networking to the third level. Team Seven helps us add layers of networks.

In the business world, networking in width is good; networking in depth is good. In the early stages, it is more profitable to work in width, but there is more security for working in depth. I prefer security over early profitability, but there are those who have built gigantic networks each way. Obviously in opening a new international market, where hundreds and often thousands of associates sign up the first day, width is preferable. After the rush is over, I prefer to return to working in depth in three teams at a time. You call it.

While working in depth is a new concept to the church, we don't need to stop our first-level networking just because we network in depth. Obviously, we always go through the first level to get to the second. It's a new concept but builds on the old.

Sometimes when a new concept comes along, you have to completely abandon the old. With Team Seven, we keep the old and build on to it. At the end of his poem, "The Journey of the Magi," T. S. Eliot compares the old and the new with the Three Wise Men, before and after meeting the Christ Child:

> All this was a long time ago, I remember,
> And I would do it again, but set down
> This set down
> This: were we led all that way for
> Birth or Death? This was a Birth, certainly,
> We had evidence and no doubt. I had seen birth and
>   death,
> But had thought they were different; this Birth was
> Hard and bitter agony for us, like Death, our death.
> We returned to our places, these Kingdoms,
> But no longer at ease here, in the old dispensation,
> With an alien people clutching their gods.
> I should be glad of another death.[1]

With Team Seven, we don't recommend that you completely abandon any previous concepts, we simply ask you to suspend any preconceived ideas as we talk.

Increasing the Harvest of the Church

So you should have put my money in the bank. Then, when
I came home, I would get my money back with interest.
                                                    —Matthew 25:27

"My money would have been better off in the bank or the
stock market," is what Jesus seems to be saying to the servant, or perhaps the church, that didn't grow. Do you recall
the story I told you in chapter 4 about the three churches
with the 7, 70, and 700 new talents respectively?

Let me show you how to take those new talents and
harvest them. The two good servants doubled their talents.
That seemed to please Jesus. So if we can double our membership, that should please Him with our work too,
shouldn't it?

Let's take a look at the 7 new members the church with
250 members got in a year. Let's see if we can take those and
create a bigger harvest. What if we could get 700? We'd have
been as effective as the church with 25,000 talents. That's
how many they got.

All I ask you to do is to keep an open mind while you are
looking at this.

I am going to show you three different ways to arrange
the seven new members and you decide which structure
is the best for the greatest harvest. Is that fair? Here are the
three I am going to show you:

1. Traditional Church Structure
2. Stacking of Leads
3. Team Seven

TRADITIONAL

Traditional is what I showed you in chapter 4. Let's review
that, now.

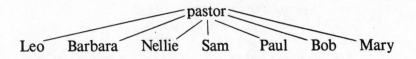

Leo   Barbara   Nellie   Sam   Paul   Bob   Mary

Please make two observations:

a. Notice that each of the seven was brought into the
   church by a different person. Nothing wrong with
   that. But that's all that is not wrong with it.

b. Notice the size of network they produced from last
   year's harvest. Let me punch the retrieve button and
   call up their networks. Here is what the computer
   shows: a blank screen. No network.

POINT MADE: If you don't plant, you don't harvest.

POINT MADE: The two types of structure introduced
next have never before in the history of the church
been used in harvesting.

POINT MADE: All we have to this point is No. 1: traditional church structure.

POINT MADE: Traditional structure is like putting a
Band-Aid on an inner tube.

STACKING

The second way of arranging the new recruits is called
stacking. It is a far cry from ideal, but it is better than traditional. Sometimes the simpleton thinks he is using Team
Seven when he is only stacking. I don't recommend this
method, but it is better than traditional.

"What if?" Even with seven different members bringing
them in, what if someone had had this information? They
could have stacked them in depth as each joined the church,
and said to them, "You are a team. We are going to teach
you the Ten Steps to Networking the Kingdom."

It would have looked like this:

> pastor
> Sam
> Nellie
> Paul
> Barbara
> Bob
> Mary
> Leo

This is not the best, but at least we can call them a team and let them go to work networking their own leads. The big problem with just stacking is that there is no glue to hold the relationships together. You, the team leader, become the glue.

Last year we didn't know to structure them like that. This year we do. This isn't bad, but it's far from the best.

Observations:

a. They are now a team, even though it is a contrived team. But at least they can function as a team.

b. There is no glue to hold the relationships together. Therefore, stacking usually doesn't stick.

c. The leader must become the glue and mold the seven into a team. Think of an audience entering the church on Sunday morning for the service. If all goes well, it is a congregation when it leaves.

d. Let's hit the retrieve button on the computer and call up the network of those we stacked. Here is what the screen shows: a small network, but larger than traditional.

POINT MADE: Stacking is weak, but stronger than traditional.

POINT MADE: Stacking is not Team Seven. It is similar only in the sense that a thermometer is similar to a thermostat.

POINT MADE: Stacking is better than traditional, but not as good as Team Seven.

POINT MADE: Stacking is a warped version of Team Seven.

POINT MADE: Stacking is used by simpletons who don't understand Team Seven.

POINT MADE: Stacking is a risky business at best and should be left to the marines' sky-divers going for a record of twenty-four vertically stacked parachutists—which, by the way, they made.

TEAM SEVEN

Do you recall the story Jesus told about planting seed in Matthew 13:3–8? Some seed didn't fare so well. But, "Some other seed fell on good ground where it grew and became grain. Some plants made 100 times more grain. Other plants made 60 times more grain, and some made 30 times more grain. You people who hear me, listen!" (Matthew 13:8–9).

We know a better way to structure to harvest the talents the Lord of the Harvest has entrusted to us—a far better way than the two we just looked at.

Team Seven is a new way of planting the seeds God has given us. We plant the seeds deep, instead of just tossing them out on the hard ground. We fertilize the seeds with Bible study and worship. We water them with our tears. When the seeds hurt, we hurt. We get the associate pastor to act as a scarecrow (just kiddin') to keep the crows and buzzards out of the vineyard. We fertilize the seeds with each other's love, and replant the seeds after the warmth of the sunshine of God's love has yielded a harvest. Amen. That's the only sermon you are going to get from me.

We now have a big, air-conditioned tractor that has a stereo headset and all the latest bells and whistles, called Team Seven, that we can use to plant and harvest with.

Just suppose that we now take each of the seven new members and begin seven new teams. For the sake of simplicity, I am going to assume that each has agreed to head up a team. We could have asked the person who brought each new member to become a leader. That would have been even better. But I am going to use the names in the illustration so you can track where we are going.

We won't call him or her the team leader, because that is a title that is earned when someone builds an in-depth team of seven new church members. If that person can't or won't be the leader, the pastor could appoint a foster sponsor as the leader. (Be sure that the head of each of the seven teams reads *Networking the Kingdom* and listens to his first six tapes before he begins.)

Right now I am going to illustrate this with Leo, Barbara, Nellie, Sam, Paul, Bob, and Mary each having a separate team and heading it up.

Now watch the fun. The seven seeds from last year's harvest look like this as we begin to pull seven seeds out of each:

Leo	Barbara	Nellie	Sam	Paul	Bob	Mary
1	1	1	1	1	1	1
2	2	2	2	2	2	2
3	3	3	3	3	3	3
4	4	4	4	4	4	4
5	5	5	5	5	5	5
6	6	6	6	6	6	6
7	7	7	7	7	7	7

(Above the columns: Pastor, connected to each of the seven names.)

From this point on, I want you to pretend that you are Mary. Everything I am saying is to you, Mary. But everything I say to you will apply to Leo, Barbara, Nellie, Sam, Paul, and Bob, the other six original seeds. I am going to teach them to do exactly what I teach you to do. But I am going to meet with them separately, so I don't confuse my readers.

To begin with, Mary, you have built your first team seven deep. It looks like this:

Pastor

Mary

1

2

3

4

5

6

7

You are now ready to build your second team the same way. But as you begin your second team, you don't abandon your first team.

As you are building your second team, go back and teach each of the new seeds or talents in your first team how to do the same thing you have done. (Just hand them this book, *Networking the Kingdom,* and the first six tapes, and let them start teaching themselves.) But while they are learning, Mary, you should keep pulling names out of them and help them to pull names out of their new seeds.

Mary, most of your team members will not yet be ready to take over all the leadership required for starting a new team. Sometimes we are tempted to "pick them green." Review chapter 12, "Transferring Leadership." Most important.

Your two teams now look something like this:

```
              Pastor
              Mary
              |
    1         1
    2         2
    3         3
    4         4
    5         5
    6         6
    7         7
```

Now build your third team the same way. Teach Team II what you taught Team I. Don't abandon Team I, or Team II. Sometimes we are tempted to go where the fire or excitement is. Make the fire go where you want it to. Make the fire go down all three teams.

Now you have completed your three teams, Mary. This sketch shows the ideal, but real networks seldom look exactly this way. By now, Team I may be thirty deep and Team II may have died.

```
              Pastor
              Mary
              |
    1         1         1
    2         2         2
    3         3         3
    4         4         4
    5         5         5
    6         6         6
    7         7         7
```

Next you go into each team and teach someone downline in each of the three teams or legs to build three teams seven deep. You may get more than one of the seven in each team to duplicate you, but it is unlikely. You must get one of the

seven or you have to keep sponsoring down until you find
someone who will duplicate your leadership in the team.
Your ideal organization would look like this:

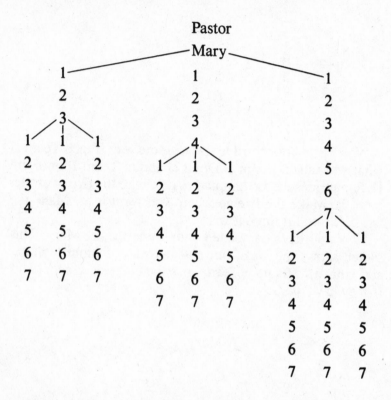

Mary, you have now built three teams seven deep with
three teams seven deep. Usually when this is done, there are
about one hundred people because some of the teams that
started earlier have considerably more than the regular
twenty-one.

That's terrific, Mary! I am going to bring Leo, Barbara,
Nellie, Sam, Paul, and Bob back into the room now because
they have been doing the same thing you have been doing.
They each have the same number of new seeds that you have.
Thanks for letting me use you as a guinea pig. Now I've got
to get back to my readers.

A Review of the Harvest Using Team Seven

At this point, each of our original seven new members has built three legs of seven (21 talents), and each of those legs has three legs of seven ($3 \times 21 = 63$). That adds up to 84 on each original new member's team ($21 + 63 = 84$). There were seven teams, so let's multiply: $7 \times 84 = 588$. Most of the teams will have between 75 (one unit) and 100 per team.

Seven teams with 100 each equals to 700 talents. That is the number of talents the church that had 25,000 brought in last year. Had the church with 25,000 gotten their 700 talents to do the same, they would have wound up with $700 \times 100 = 70,000$.

We figured conservatively, using one person per team member, when in actuality the average family, which counts as one team member, has three members. If you want to really see something, multiply the above results for each church by three.

Conclusions:

POINT MADE: Team Seven has good relationship glue.

POINT MADE: Team Seven generates leads.

POINT MADE: Team Seven encourages the developing of new leaders.

POINT MADE: Team Seven grows empires and dynasties.

POINT MADE: Team Seven doesn't work if we don't.

POINT MADE: Team Seven is not held back by weaknesses in certain team members, because another strong member can pick up and go on.

POINT MADE: Team Seven produces new seeds.

POINT MADE: Let's hit the retrieve button and see the harvest using Team Seven: The original 7 seeds have now produced 700. We only were looking to double. We grew by 100 times. The church with 2,500 talents shows 7,000 talents. The church with 25,000 talents shows 70,000 talents.

POINT MADE: Team Seven works when we do.

POINT MADE: Even if we killed ourselves working twenty-four hours a day, traditional structure and stacking could produce only piddling results compared to Team Seven.

POINT MADE: Traditional structure and stacking are to Team Seven what a water pistol is to a cannon.

POINT MADE: The Lord of the Harvest must be pleased with our new vehicle: Team Seven, streamlined and designed to network the kingdom.

POINT MADE: Traditional and stacking are to Team Seven what a horse and buggy are to a jet fighter plane. Anyone can just piddle around with a horse and buggy with little or no training or experience. But if you decide to fly a jet fighter plane, you had best learn everything you can before you take the controls, because a jet was not designed for piddling around. Once you pull back on the throttle, it's going somewhere and you're going with it. Once you set Team Seven in motion, it's going somewhere and you are going with it. You can't get the genie back into the bottle. Team Seven goes to and through networks like a jet goes through the sound barrier.

POINT MADE: Taking a hint from "The Three Little Pigs," we can sum up the three types of structure this way:

1. Traditional—straw
2. Stacking—sticks
3. Team Seven—BRICK

Curse the Darkness or Light a Candle

Do you remember the story of the little boy who was holding a bird in his hand? He had finally trapped the wise man.

The boy said, "Is the bird dead or alive?" He knew if the wise man said, "Alive," he could crush the bird to death. If he said, "Dead," he could let the bird fly away.

The wise man looked at the boy for a moment and replied, "The decision is in your hand."

I don't know what you will do with Team Seven. As is true in most of life, we have two basic choices in any area: We can "curse the darkness," or we can "light a candle."

Now that we know about Team Seven, we have two options. We can throw rocks at the concept and say it doesn't work, or we can get started. We can, like the foolish servant, hide the talents the Lord of the Harvest has entrusted to us; or we can begin planting the seeds and buying more land (I meant parking spaces) for our greatest harvest. Oh. I know they are only numbers. But a few minutes ago, even the numbers weren't in our minds. Wasn't it Napoleon Hill who said, "Anything the mind of man can conceive and believe, the mind of a man can achieve"? Wasn't it God who gave us our minds?

Well, now we've conceived it. I can't think of any reason Jesus wouldn't want us to grow. It seems that all that is necessary is for us to believe that *we* and He can do it, and get after it.

What if it did work? It won't if we don't. We guarantee its failure in our church by not attempting it.

I tell my business recruits, "We'd sue another person who did to our businesses what we do to them ourselves. We guarantee that every prospect we ever meet will say, 'No,' if we don't approach them."

Same thing down at the church. If we don't contact the prospects, how in the world do we think they are going to respond, favorably or otherwise?

7
Leverage

et's you and I dream a dream of "What if?" You see, it
doesn't take many team leaders to make a tremendous
impact. If we could just find three, and we helped them each
build three teams seven deep, with three teams each seven
deep, we'd add about 300 to our memberships. If you don't
dream, how can you expect your dreams to come true?

You see, it's not the size of the church; it's the size of the
dream. Remember the old saying, "It's not the size of the dog
in the fight, it's the size of the fight in the dog." Surely, you
and I could find three who would dream a dream of "What
if?" Many people go through their whole lives saying, "If I
had a church as big as so and so, I'd do such and such. You
don't understand my situation here at this place. Maybe
that'd happen in Dallas, Texas, but not Ooltewah, Tennessee. I've got a little bitty church in a little bitty town. If
only . . ." Their whole conversation is based on, "Before I
came . . . ," "Since I came . . . ," or "Since I left. . . ."

When I was a boxer in the Golden Gloves in Cleveland,
Tennessee, our coach told us this story.

He said, "The heavyweight champion of the world went on a tour of the country. Everywhere he went, someone would say to him something like this: 'Boy, if I were as big and strong as you are, I'd go out in the woods and grab the biggest black bear I could find. I'd tear him limb from limb.'

"The champ got so tired of people saying, 'If this, and if that,' that he told his manager he wanted to cancel his trip.

"The wise manager said, 'The next time someone says that to you, tell them there are some little bears out there, too.'"

Do you see the difference that you and I could make if instead of saying "If I were" we said "What if I?" What if we dreamed the "possible dream" instead of the "impossible"?

Why Don't I Just Go Out and Get Seven of My Friends to Join the Church?

I am going to answer this woman's question. Let's call her Sally, with seven friends. But first I want you to know that it may appear to you that I am just going over the information I gave you in chapter 6. I am, but with a couple of very subtle nuances. You will track with me much faster now, though.

I want to do this because this situation will come up many times, and it is a good question.

Notice the difference in this illustration and the illustration I used with the seven new talents in the story of the church and the talents.

1. In the first story, the seven talents were brought by seven different church members.

2. Sally, with seven friends, is bringing all seven herself. You can already see that there is at least a little glue there.

3. In both instances, the church is still at the first level of networking.

What do you say to Sally when she says, "Why don't I just go out and get seven of my friends to join the church?" Let's answer that question now.

First of all, we know Sally has not completely understood the concept. Let's at least acknowledge that if she brings in

seven of her friends, that is great. But that is sort of like
packing a pew, and there is very little glue. There is no team
to hold them together.

The worst thing about it is that even if Sally gets seven of
her friends, the church is still first-level networking, or only
one network deep. We still have only leads provided by a
current church member.

If you fail to see this, and many do, you may never penetrate the other layers of prospects. What we want to do is to
penetrate Sally's friends' networks, layer by layer. That turns
her seven leads into $7 \times 75 = 525$ new networks to be penetrated for the church. That 525 would make a fairly large-
sized church.

There are four alternatives for arranging Sally's seven
friends. See which you like best.

1. First, if we did it the traditional way, which is the
weakest method because we get no leverage, no leads, and
no glue, her prospects would look like this:

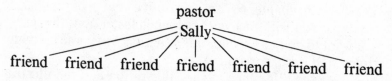

pastor

Sally

friend   friend   friend   friend   friend   friend   friend

2. The second possibility is a little better: Make seven
teams, seven deep. Her group would now look like this:

pastor

Sally

friend	friend	friend	friend	friend	friend	friend
2	2	2	2	2	2	2
3	3	3	3	3	3	3
4	4	4	4	4	4	4
5	5	5	5	5	5	5
6	6	6	6	6	6	6
7	7	7	7	7	7	7

3. That would be fantastic, but I recommend a third arrangement, which is better, but not yet the best. Build three teams, using only three of Sally's friends to head each team. Even like this, I recommend that Sally not try to build a second team until she has her first team seven deep.

After she builds her first team seven deep, then she starts her second, and so on. After she has built three teams seven deep, I suggest that she help them build their three teams seven deep, a very important point, rather than starting legs four, five, and six with her other four friends.

```
                        pastor
                   ┌────── Sally ──────┐
                   │         │          │
  friend one          friend two        friend three
        2                  2                 2
        3                  3                 3
     ╱  3  ╲               4                 4
   1    1    1          ╱  4  ╲              5
   2    2    2        1    1    1           6
   3    3    3        2    2    2           7
   4    4    4        3    3    3        ╱  7  ╲
   5    5    5        4    4    4      1    1    1
   6    6    6        5    5    5      2    2    2
   7    7    7        6    6    6      3    3    3
                      7    7    7      4    4    4
                                      5    5    5
                                      6    6    6
                                      7    7    7
```

The bad part about waiting that long for friends four, five, six, and seven to start a team is that by the time Sally is ready to help them, they will probably have lost interest.

Now, let's look at the fourth way of structuring Sally's seven friends in order to get the greatest harvest, using leverage.

Leverage: Structure

If I had a lever long enough, I could lift the world.

—Archimedes

Most people think that salesmen are the best people at networking. They are on the low end of the spectrum. A salesman's greatest asset becomes his biggest weakness. Let me illustrate. A salesman talks to someone about a subject. The non-salesman is thinking, "I could never do that well." So if you're a salesman, don't be so good. Play the salesman part down a little. Speak a little softer, slower, and lower. Only five percent of most audiences would be salesmen or saleswomen; the other ninety-five percent would not.

Guess what profession the highest paid networkers belong to? Nope. Engineers! The people who have the highest incomes and largest networks are engineers.

I don't know why. But I think it may be because of their understanding of that little word *leverage*. They also understand the importance of structure in attaining leverage.

Do you remember Archimedes? He's the one who said, "If I had a lever long enough, I could lift the world."

4. Let me show you the fourth and best way to arrange Sally's seven friends so that Sally and the church get the most leverage. She doesn't need to tell her friends how she is arranging them. It is only important that they agree to be somewhere on her team.

I am going to tell you what we are going to do, and then we'll do it. We're going to place one of Sally's friends just under her and pull two or three names out of him or his friends. Looks like this:

> pastor
> Sally
> Sally's first friend
> friend of first friend
> friend of first friend's friend
> friend of first friend's friend's friend

Notice that so far we have placed only one of Sally's friends on the team. We pulled the other leads out of Sally's first friend's recruits. That's leverage. As long as we are pulling names out of the others, we don't need to put a "gimme" in there. But in order to get the team going faster, let's go ahead and bring in Sally's second friend, who is waiting in the wings. We already have him reading *Networking the Kingdom* and listening to his first six tapes. He's the "gimme." (That's a term used in playing marbles. It means someone "gives me" a marble.) He's chomping at the bit to get going, and says, "This thing is going to be a piece of cake. I don't need you folks. I can get my team by myself."

He can't. But it's okay that he thinks he can. Be careful that you don't let your team members talk this thing to death. Don't ever give them a platform for "What I'm going to do." But let them have the run of the stage to say "What I did and how I did it."

He goes in as Sally's fifth team member even though he is her second original friend. This is my best stuff. Stay with me now. I'm on a roll. Sally, with seven friends, is also. Looks like this now:

Sally's First Team

> pastor
> Sally
> Sally's first friend
> friend of first friend
> friend of first friend's friend
> friend of first friend's friend's friend
> Sally's second original friend
> Second friend's friend
> Second friend's friend's friend

So far, we have leveraged only Sally's first and second original friends and already have Team I, seven deep. Team I keeps going, but now Sally starts Team II and builds it the same way using original friends three and four as the building blocks.

Team II keeps going. Sally starts her third team with original friends five, six, and seven. They have been reading *Networking the Kingdom* and almost have it memorized, and say, "We can do it." Sally wants this team to really fire out, so she leverages it like this:

Sally's Third Team

pastor
Sally
friend five
friend five's friend
friend six
friend six's friend
friend seven
friend seven's friend
one of the above's friend

Sally could put this team together in a week because the others already had their prospects scouted out and they, too, were waiting in the wings.

Now Sally gets a couple of team leaders in each of her three legs to build three legs each the same way.

How 'bout that? Couldn't be done.

Which one of the four types of structure do you think is the most effective? That's a no-brainer, isn't it?

Leverage: Time

In the business world we often speak of O.P.M., which means Other People's Money. In Team Seven, we speak of O.P.T., Other People's Time. If you are a staff member, campus leader, evangelist, or missionary, you only have so many hours a week that you can effectively minister. But "What if?"

What if you had one team member who recruited seven team members and they each made a commitment to devote four hours a week to membership recruiting (two Coffee Shop Meetings and two lunches)? Four hours a week × 50 weeks in a year = 200 hours. Now let's say the average age is thirty-five, and each is going to network the kingdom the rest of his or her active life, say another forty years. Two hundred hours per year per team member × 40 years = 8,000 lifetime hours. Now, 8,000 hours a year per person × 8 (team leader and 7 team members) = 64,000 leveraged hours.

If one team leader with a team of seven members can produce 64,000 hours in a lifetime, how many teams of seven would an organization need? And surely during those forty years someone would sponsor someone else. What if each of the eight just got one? Staggering, isn't it?

That's how you leverage time for the kingdom using the Team Seven concept.

Retention

One of the problems in the local church is retention. After a time, members just slip away or become inactive. Team Seven eliminates a great deal of this. How?

Do you think Sally, or any of the other team members, is going to get her feelings hurt and go off and leave the church, or do you think team members are going to be the first ones there on Sunday morning to welcome their teams? (We might call team leaders who get seventy-five, one unit, the "pastor's assistants." What do you think?)

Remember the Rule of Seven. When anyone makes seven friends in a church, he or she is not likely to leave the church. How much stronger the roots if he introduced the seven to the church.

Do you know how you keep a nut from coming off a bolt? You screw another nut on behind it. Now, I'm not calling you a nut, but by the time you get seven nuts on there, that first nut is not coming off. The seventh one might come off, but not the first.

Focus

Another thing Team Seven does is help you focus. If you have Sally's seven friends spread out the way we showed you in the traditional structure, it's like yodeling in a canyon.

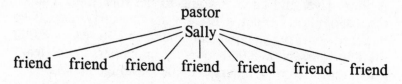

pastor

Sally

friend friend friend friend friend friend friend

You work with one of Sally's friends for about thirty days. Then you go over and help her second friend get a team started. When you get back over to the first, he is discouraged and has quit. You go over and work with Sally's third friend and her husband for a month. When you get back over to the second friend, he's lost interest.

It's like that entertainer that we see on TV sometimes who spins the plates. He does a whole act trying to keep all the plates spinning.

You can take a magnifying glass and get it angled just right with the sun, and burn a hole in a coffee table. But if you move the magnifying glass around the room, it creates no heat, and the erratic flashes of light only get in the onlookers' eyes and irritate them.

If you concentrate on one team at a time, you can put a team of seven together very quickly. Team Seven goes like a jet stream, zoom! Traditional structure is like a wagon wheel and takes years.

How old is your church? Let's say it is fifty years old. If we can double in size in a year, using Team Seven, wouldn't that mean that Team Seven goes fifty times faster than the other?

Learn from the Pros

Learn from the pros in networking. One of the largest networking companies has nearly two million distributors in its network. It is built on only five legs or teams. Of course some of their people downline have more, but the corporation itself only has five lines.

The Pentagon has five. The entire military teaches management of three to five lines. All of business says that you can effectively manage only three to five organizations.

Such being the case, I recommend that you build three teams, one at a time. Build deep first and wide second. Depth promotes teamwork and harmony. Width often promotes the opposite. If there is anything the church is going to need from all these new members, it is going to be teamwork and harmony.

Your Team Is Already Intact

If it ever dawns on you that your team is already intact out there, and your doubled or tripled church is already out there in existence, your spouse will think you have gotten a new lease on life. Your team can't contact you. They don't even know you. Team Seven leads you to and through them. See in every person a network of friends.

Once you see this, you'll run and not walk. You'll work and not grow weary, and you won't faint.

Until you do, any old brother-in-law can steal it from you by saying, "It won't work." Any old excuse will do, if you choose not to do it.

But you can do it. I know you can. What if it did work? What if it only worked half that well? What if you just grew by fifty percent? Would that be so bad?

Team Seven Does Not Alter Your Present Witnessing Style

All Team Seven does is help you locate and recruit the prospect for the kingdom. It does not alter your style of witnessing, your techniques of visitation, training, or ministry to prospects.

If you have no style or techniques for recruiting prospects, we suggest some, just to get you going. Many church members are overtrained anyway. If you have people skills, use them. If you don't, get some.

I am going to illustrate to you that you know enough right now that you can get a friend to a Coffee Shop Meeting or to a Sunday morning worship service this coming Sunday. I don't care who you are. I am going to show you that you can do it. I guarantee it. How?

Let me illustrate this using the morning worship service, although I could use the Coffee Shop Meeting just as well.

Here's the deal: If you knew that this coming Sunday Jesus Christ Himself was going to be at your church and was going to be delivering the message, could you get someone there? I mean, if you knew it. If it were the headline in every major newspaper and all the TV and radio talk-show hosts were talking about it:

JESUS CHRIST, LORD OF HEAVEN, TO DELIVER MESSAGE SUNDAY
AT
CROSS ROADS FRIENDLY CHURCH

"What if? What if you knew Jesus was going to be there and deliver the message, could you get someone there?"

You say, "Of course I could, if Jesus were going to be there. Who couldn't?"

Now we know that you know how to get someone to church. We just haven't convinced you that the "prize is worth the price" to get you to get someone there. It should be obvious to both you and me that you know everything you need to know right now.

You say, "But you tricked me."

Yes. Sort of. I had you play a game of "What if?"

By the way, this was not entirely a game. You see, Jesus will be there Sunday morning for the morning worship service. And He will be delivering the message through your pastor.

The Gifts

The new members at your church will be much more accepting of the Team Seven concept than will some of your more conservative membership. Watch out for those who say to you, "Mine is the gift of speaking and warning others."

I heard about three spiritual giants who were bitter enemies and were all on the same program, God only knows why. The first head of a major faction got up and said, "God has given me the gift of prophecy . . . thus and thus. . . ."

The second head got up and said, "God has given me the gift of speaking and warning . . . thus and thus. . . ."

The third head got up and said, "God has given me the gift of discernment, and you're both liars."

Who would deny that God gives gifts to certain people? All I am saying is that when a brother or sister starts using his "gifts" as a club, be careful. Watch out.

If you are currently a church member and are not a caring person, Team Seven is not likely to make you more caring. If you have good skills in the area of bonding and helping people get involved in your church, you will have a field day with Team Seven. I was explaining Team Seven at a meeting for a church. (That was before I learned not to present the concept to a group.) One pious soul got up and said, with a little acid in his voice, "God gave me the gift of speaking and warning. It looks like all you are doing is running a bunch of people through the church. When I bring a new person to this church, I care for him and teach him."

How we say things and how we respond reveal so much. Are you ever tempted to respond in kind? Yeah, me too. But I didn't. I said, "That's what we want all of our people to do. But they may not all have as much skill at it as you do. What you are doing is working so well; you may not need to use Team Seven."

The pastor jumped up and said, "Folks, last year we grew from 250 to 257. We're not exactly running people through the church all that fast. We're trained. We know what to do. We just don't have the people to do it to and with."

The same fellow got back up and said, still with acid in his voice, "Doesn't the term 'networking' have a bad connotation?"

I wanted to say, "I don't come down to your place of

business and break up the cue sticks." But I didn't. I said, "Well, Sears has the Sears Network. C.B.S. has the C.B.S. Network. A lot of large companies market their products through networking. John Naisbitt likes the term. The Harvard School of Business likes it. I am sure there are those who have abused it."

Then I said, "By the way, sir, what do you do for a living?"

To which he replied, "I'm a used car salesman."

Everyone else was positive, but that fellow had a burr under his saddle. But in spite of the acid and the burr, his were good, legitimate questions.

I told you how I felt like responding, so you'll know that when you feel that way, it's okay. It's normal to feel that way, but we had better not express those feelings out loud. That is called responding in kind.

When someone asks you a question about Team Seven, filter out the emotions, both his and yours. Everyone has his or her own agenda. I think the key is this: Act; don't react.

On any subject or product, if people don't ask questions, they have no interest. Welcome the questions. But do your damage control in private. If you have someone who threatens to become a real troublemaker, don't give that person a platform. Deal with him or her in private. You don't pet a rattlesnake. With some people, you would sooner have a rattlesnake in your bosom than have one of them in your inner circle of kingdom networkers. Enough said.

I think that what we all have to do is use the concept, and not get too legalistic or dogmatic. Be flexible with it. We as denominations agree on many things, but we allow each other to have our own interpretation of what God is saying to us in His Word. Let's also let each other interpret what He is saying, if anything, about Team Seven as we go about networking the kingdom.

> One who is too insistent on his own views,
> finds few to agree with him.
>
> —Lao-Tsu, Tao Teh King

Team Seven Is Similar to a "Slinky" Toy

Team Seven is similar to a "Slinky" toy, except in one respect. If you set a "Slinky" at the top of a set of steps, it will continue to descend until it lands at the bottom of the last step.

Team Seven, like the "Slinky," also descends through steps of networks until it reaches the bottom of the network. Ah! But here is where the similarities between Team Seven and a "Slinky" toy end. The "Slinky" stops at the last landing. Team Seven drills to and through the next network like a laser beam going through steel. It goes on into infinity.

8
Ten Steps to Networking the Kingdom

> But let everything be done in a way that is right and orderly.
> —I Corinthians 14:40

I heard someone say one time, "The worst thing you can do is get people excited about a new product, concept, or business venture, and then not tell them how and what to do with it."

This information is for the team leader or new team member who wishes to become a team leader. Obviously, we want every new team member to become a team leader. But we know that only twenty percent of them will. Since we do not know which ones will be in the twenty percent, we teach the Ten Steps to everyone.

It is important that you do all ten steps. You don't have to, but if you don't, an important element will be missing. I tell my people, "You can drive from Dallas to Fort Worth with only three tires on your car, but it's a rough ride. You might run into a ditch and hurt yourself or someone else. It's best if you use four tires. It's best if you use all Ten Steps."

Step 1: Make a List of Twenty Names

Make a list of twenty names of people you know who are unchurched. Your first question is probably, "How do I know whether they are or not?" Assume they are not unless you know for certain that they are. If you were making a list of potential customers to whom you were going to try to sell vacuum cleaners or encyclopedias, you would call on them first. They will tell you if they already have your product.

Someone might say, "But here at the church we are not selling anything." Maybe so, maybe not. You are approaching people, and you can't approach them until you think of them. And the best way to think of them is to have them on your list. We are doing on purpose what we used to do by accident.

Remember what I tell my business associates: We'd sue a competitor who does to our business what we do to it ourselves. If we do not make a list and do not call on our clients, by neglect we force all of them to refuse our product or service. If the preacher were saying this to us, he'd probably say, "These are sins of omission."

Do you feel that there is some of that element among our church membership? By not asking our friends and acquaintances to visit our church, we are forcing them to say no. Of course they might say no if we ask them, but they all say the equivalent of no if we don't ask them.

I was teaching the Team Seven concept to one church, and when the pastor asked for questions, one man stood and said, "All of my acquaintances are already church members. I've been in the church all my life, and I just don't know anyone who is not in church." (Again, this was before I learned not to present the concept to even a selected large group.) The pastor asked me to comment on that.

This fellow had been lulled to sleep by getting all of his thinking from the church. He honestly thought this. If the truth were known, this is probably the thinking of eighty percent of the best people in the church.

I said to the group, "Isn't this the way most of us feel after having been raised in the church? Most of our associations are with those who are already churched. We just don't run around with that other crowd too much. And if we do, we don't want anyone to know it." Most laughed in agreement.

Then I said, "Let's look a little closer. Who carries your mail? Is he attending church? How about your golf pro at the country club? Your service station attendant? The woman who checks you out at the grocery store? Your dentist? Your son's coach?"

YOU CAN HAVE TOO MANY NAMES ON YOUR PROSPECT LIST

I was speaking at a national convention for network marketers in California. I said, "You can have too many names on your prospect list." You could hear the gasps from some in the audience.

Sounds like a paradox, doesn't it? You see, some had not yet comprehended the economy of pulling names from the prospects who had become their new associates. They had missed another important element here. That is the value of the glue of relationships that is found in pulling the names of their new prospects from their new associates or old prospects who decided not to join them.

All you need are a couple of names. After you sponsor them as new team members, you work out of their network. That is what takes the church through seven layers of networks. If you just stacked your seven friends one under the other, you would never have left your own network. Thus you are forcing the church to continue to operate out of its present contacts, which is first-level networking.

PULLING NAMES FROM YOUR TEAM MEMBERS

Not all team members will give you a name. If they don't, it's because they don't know what you (and others that you might turn the name over to) are going to do with or to their friends. After their confidence is up, they'll introduce you to all of their friends.

Therefore, tell Joe to keep his list that he makes up. They are his friends. Always let him keep his list. His list is to fertilize his brain, not ours. If all we needed was a list, we could use the telephone directory. What we need from Joe is his influence to recruit his network.

Don't dally too long on any one team member or prospect who isn't ready to go. We're looking for those who want to ride the Team Seven Gospel Train right now. We'll be back later, but this train has a coffee shop schedule to keep and we have "miles to go before we sleep." Wow! Did I say that?

If they aren't ready to join our team or help us build a team now, we'll just put them on our "I'll get you yet" list. We'll be patient and consistent, but we won't bug them.

Step 2: Get a Pocket or Purse Calendar

The reason you are going to need a pocket calendar is that you are going to set appointments for Coffee Shop Meetings. You want to have your calendar with you or in reach at all times. Keep your gun loaded, so to speak.

Every now and then someone will say, "My secretary keeps my calendar." I understand that. If such is the case, get a pocket or purse calendar and have your secretary block out times in it that are yours, times that you schedule and he or she doesn't.

When you ask someone to go to coffee with you to discuss Team Seven, you are probably going to be asking that person in a casual setting, such as at work or in the car. It is too formal and too cumbersome to have to say, "I'll check my schedule and get back with you." That's the prospect's line, not yours. If you have your calendar in your purse or pocket, you can say, "How about Friday morning at 10:00 at the Anatole Hotel, Chanticleer's Coffee Shop?"

You understand why I was so specific about the name of the restaurant in the hotel. The Anatole has two registration lobbies and at least six restaurants. Be specific. I had an actress wait an hour for me in the wrong lobby at the Anatole Hotel. I didn't tell her it had two lobbies and which one. Fortunately, she had me paged.

Step 3: Read Networking the Kingdom and Listen to Your First Six Tapes

When you decided to become a team member, you were given, or you purchased, a copy of *Networking the Kingdom* and six tapes.

You are a new team member and are ready to get started. We are ready for you to get started, too. But there is some important information you need to digest before beginning. We want you to be as "wise as serpents, and harmless as doves" (Matthew 10:16, King James Version).

Before you talk to anyone, we want you to listen to your first six tapes and read *Networking the Kingdom*. Why? At this point, you are like a "babe in the woods" so far as this concept is concerned. Remember, "there are none so righteous as the newly converted." But we want you to be trained, too.

Sometimes in our enthusiasm we want to "storm the gates of Hell with a water pistol." We say, "If you are going to do this, let's at least get you a battleworthy weapon and teach you how to load it, how to aim it and who to aim it at." Of course, we all know that prayer is the ultimate battle weapon.

GO SLOW SO YOU CAN GO FAST

I tell my new business recruits that we want them to go slowly so they can go fast. I say, "If Jesus spent thirty years preparing and three years ministering, it's not a bad example for us."

Most stock brokerage houses tell their new recruits studying for their licenses, "We will fire you if you talk with anyone during your six-month training period." In fact, it is even against the law for them to do so.

If it is that important in the business world, how much more important should training be for networking the kingdom?

We want to give you a head start. In a marathon race, it is more fun to be a half a mile ahead than to be a half a mile behind trying to catch up.

Step 4: Automatic Shipment of a Tape Each Month

It is important that you participate in the Automatic Shipment Program. This means you are on Automatic Shipment for one tape a month. These tapes will keep you current on all the latest developments in the concept. They will also feature outstanding church leaders who are explaining how the concept is being used in their situations and the results they are getting. We will make every effort to keep the tapes from becoming theologically slanted. They will deal only with the implementation of Team Seven. We will learn from each other.

The reason we earlier recommended that you read the book and listen to your first six tapes on networking the kingdom is that this bit of information gets you from the side streets onto the main streets, and then on out of town to the interstate highway.

But the Automatic Shipment Program of a tape each month "locks you in" on the interstate highway, and keeps you from running into a ditch or getting sidetracked. We are going on a long, wonderfully exciting journey together. It is the journey that we will be emphasizing and not the destination. The Automatic Shipment Program is our road map.

Things work better when they are plugged in and Tape of the Month plugs you in. By plugging into the wall plug, you connect up to an available power source. By plugging into

Tape of the Month, you plug into all the available information on Team Seven.

Even the best woodsman has to sharpen his axe every now and then. If he doesn't, his axe gets dull, and soon he isn't getting much work done. At that point, he either gets his axe sharpened, buys another axe, or quits. Tapes sharpen your axe.

Step 5: Learn an Effective Approach for Setting an Appointment

Old recipe for tiger stew: "First you must catch the tiger."

You can't score if you can't get on first base. If you can't set the appointment, you can't get the sale. You can't make the tiger stew until you catch the tiger. So sell the appointment, not the product.

When you approach someone to invite him or her to have coffee or Perrier water with you, there are things you can say that make it easier to get the appointment. It's like asking a girl for a date. There are ways to ask and ways not to ask. Solomon said:

A word fitly spoken is like
apples of gold in pictures of silver.
—Proverbs 25:11 (King James Version)

You may already be skilled at setting appointments, but your team members will have to be taught. You don't want to leave them without guidance in this area.

Sometimes someone says, "I already know how to invite people to church. Why do I need to go to coffee with them to do it?"

That brother or sister is still "packing a pew." Inviting someone to church and inviting someone to a Coffee Shop Meeting are similar.

Team Seven is as different from the regular church visitation program as a thermostat is from a thermometer.

They are similar. Both have to do with the same thing, but both serve different purposes. The thermometer shows how hot it is, and the thermostat gets it hot. Team Seven gets it hot!

The Coffee Shop Meeting is a step from nothing to something. It is a way to remove some of the confrontation that some church leaders have touted as "the way." It also gives you a chance to sell your prospect on the church.

If you can get them to church by simply inviting them to church, you can certainly get them there by having a Coffee Shop Meeting first. The converse is not true. One works seventy percent of the time and the other works thirty percent of the time.

I heard a speaker tell the story of a new convert at a church. He was still a little rough around the edges and very uncouth, but he had great enthusiasm. He bugged the pastor to death wanting a place of service in the church.

Finally the pastor, thinking he was giving enough instruction, said, "Okay. Here are the names of ten inactive church members. Some are prominent citizens of the town. Here is some church stationery. See if you can get them back to church."

The new convert accepted the challenge.

About three weeks after the letters went out, the church received a letter from a prominent physician in the city. His name had been on the list. Inside the letter was a check for one thousand dollars and this note:

Dear Preacher:

Enclosed is my check for one thousand dollars to make up for my missing church so much. But be assured that I will be present this coming Lord's Day and each Lord's Day following. I will not, by choice, miss services again.

Sincerely,

M. B. Jones, M.D.

P.S. Would you please tell your secretary that there is only one 't' in *dirty,* and no 'c' in *skunk.*

While he was effective, I think we can get some words that are a little more duplicatable and palatable. What do you think?

THE 70-30 RULE

The 70-30 Rule is a truth in business. Here it is: If you use an effective approach, seventy percent of the time you will get the appointment. If you use an ineffective approach, you will get the appointment only thirty percent of the time.

That is why in my business, I do not trust my billfold with a new distributor. What does that mean? It means I don't make any money unless my distributor does, and he can't make as much money if he is only thirty percent effective. My goal is to start him at seventy percent effectiveness.

No one can get appointments one hundred percent of the time, but why force failure? Do you remember the statement I used earlier, "A wise man learns from the experience of others; a fool ought to learn from his own experience"?

How do you teach a new person to get seventy percent of his appointments? Teach him a canned approach. Write it down and have him read it back to you while you are training him. Insist that he use it on the first seven people he calls. After that, he can put it into his own words.

You can use this while teaching your Team Seven members. If they are trying to set appointments and are not getting the appointments, you know they are not using the approach you taught them. In their head, they may think they are, but sometimes they are only using the approach they thought you taught them.

Do you remember the game "Gossip" we played when we were younger? We'd get in a circle. Someone would be assigned to whisper a secret to the person next to him, and that person would whisper the secret to the next, and so on. By the time it got to you, you were supposed to say the secret out loud. Everyone laughed because it had been altered so, and by the time it got to you, it was hardly recognizable.

You see, we all have our hidden agenda in our brains and

beings. I have my new associates call me to practice their approach on me. If they do not have it written out, they think they are saying what I taught them. But it is usually so different that it is ineffective.

After whatever chitchat you have done, whether in person or on the phone, use something like this:

Joe, let's get together for coffee one day this next week. I've got something I want to run by you.

or

Don, our friend Joe, the mechanic, gave me your name and suggested we might get together for a cup of coffee. He's a new friend of mine and wanted us to get together. We've got a couple of things we'd like to run by you, but nothing to do with making money or raising money. How does Tuesday at 5:30 at the Golden Corral Steak House sound for a cup of coffee? Joe said he'd buy.

or

Sue, I've got something I want to run by you, and it has nothing to do with making money, spending money, or business, [but it could do you, our community, and local church a lot of good]. I don't know if you would be interested, but I'd like to get with you over a cup of coffee and explain it to you.

If you feel uncomfortable with the phrase in brackets, just omit that and use the rest of the approach. I know that you can think of a dozen approaches better than these. Use yours. If you can't, modify one of mine and use it. But before you criticize mine, be fair, and write yours down and analyze it. Just speaking it is not a fair comparison. Write it down, and see if you would want to teach it to all your future network.

I will not let you discuss mine with me until you have written yours down and handed it to me, so I can see what you said, not what you thought you said. Big difference. Mine are not written in stone. Just suggestions.

If one of your team members doesn't like these, don't let him sit around and whine about it. Tell him to do one of his own. But make him write it down and turn it in to you, so you can see what is being taught downline in your network.

If you can't think of a better one, use one of my suggestions. It makes no difference to me whether you use them or not. It should matter to you, that you not give the platform to some malcontent and let him sit around in front of your group and argue over whether or not he is going to use one of these. Watch out for would-be preachers who are looking for a platform. Use one of my suggestions or don't use them, and go on.

"Why did we not tell Joe everything we wanted to talk with him about?" If we told him everything, there wouldn't be a need for us to meet, would there? Don't you agree that we can tell him about our church better in person than on the phone? Telling him about it on the phone is sort of like watching color TV on the phone, isn't it?

We've told him enough that he knows generally what we want to talk to him about.

Ezra Pound, the poet's poet, said, "Curiosity is the wellspring of creativity." We don't want to carry that too far, but it is a good marketing technique.

If I offend you by talking to you about business principles used in setting appointments, I apologize for offending you, but not for talking to you about them. Jesus had a lot to say about business principles. You might want to review the story of the talents in chapter 5, and in Matthew 25:14–30.

In *The Greatest Salesman in the World,* Og Mandino tells one of the most touching stories I have ever read. It brings tears to your eyes and joy to your heart. Do you remember who was selected to receive the scrolls? Ah! You are arguing with yourself if you think the gospel doesn't use business principles. Mr. Mandino says:

Even the Word of God must be sold to the people or they will hear it not.[1]

If I were a used car salesman, I'd talk to you about low mileage, and little old ladies who drive the cars only on Sundays, and clutches.

If I were a preacher, I'd talk with you about exegesis, isagogics, preterition, the rapture, and pre- and postmillennialism or something. I'm not; I can't; so I won't.

I have to speak to you in terms that I understand. I am a pedagogue. I am an average salesman but a superior teacher. I am an average composer, but an above average conductor. But of any talents I have, I am better at networking and teaching networking than I am at anything else I do. It was made for me.

I was teaching you an approach to use when you call a prospect. It's one thing if you are calling one of your friends. But it's a horse of a different color when you pick up the phone to call Don, the dentist, whom you have never met, and who is a friend of Joe, the mechanic.

I GOT SO SCARED ON MY FIRST PHONE CALL THAT I HUNG UP

I recall when I first got into network marketing. Now, I was already a pretty successful businessman. I owned an Air Force Base and a Hilton Hotel, and I had been a Full Professor with tenure, and Division Chairman at a university. I called this very important person to tell him about my business. When he answered, I got so scared, I hung up the first two times I called him.

I became speechless and tongue-tied. I did not have a written-out speech to guide me. I couldn't remember my name, much less his. I gasped, coughed, turned red in the face and then white, and that phone felt like it weighed a ton; I knew it would break my foot if I dropped it. So I hung up.

I felt like the lady I heard about who had an asthma attack during an obscene phone call.

The caller said, "Did I call you or did you call me?"

Now, folks, I'm at least average. And networking the kingdom is at least as important as my other business. Let's acknowledge that it doesn't hurt to give our people some words to lean on when they call their prospects. I know that you are different, but your people aren't.

When we call a friend, it's different. But even if we have the gift of gab, when we call a friend of Joe, the mechanic, Don, the dentist, whom we have never met, we sometimes lose it.

For the most part, the only way we will lose a new team member is if, when he makes his first call, he feels like he blew it. If he fails here, his network may be gone forever. He must get a little success here. Not much, but a little. He's got to get a "single," even if he has to bunt. But he's got to get on base, or he may just go watch TV.

CONTACT TAPE

For our business associates who feel they do not have the posture to contact certain people on their list, we furnish a generic Contact Tape. They hand the five-minute overview tape to the prospect and let him listen to it. The tape only sells the concept being offered and not the product.

With Team Seven, we have a five-minute Contact Tape on *Networking the Kingdom.* (See the Appendix.) It is generic and simply explains what we would cover with a prospect on the phone.

You say to your prospect, "Sally, I'd like to get with you over a cup of coffee, but to see if you might be interested, I'd like to leave this five-minute tape with you so you'll know what I want to talk with you about."

You leave the tape with her and tell her you'll pick it up in forty-eight hours. When you pick up the tape, say, "Why don't we get together over a cup of coffee and discuss the tape?" If you hand out five Contact Tapes a week, you might build your team seven deep in two weeks.

POINT MADE: The contact tape is one hundred percent duplicatable. The phone call approach is seventy percent duplicatable. The confrontation or traditional method is thirty percent duplicatable.

If Don, the dentist, says no to his invitation, Joe, the mechanic, is going to feel he failed, anyway. We don't want him to be kicking himself because he wasn't prepared. We can accept a prospect's saying, "No." We just can't accept its being our fault that they said, "No." Using the Contact Tape, we can at least blame the tape.

BE PREPARED

All I am saying is, "Be prepared." We teach our young people to decide in advance what they will do and say in certain situations. Remember the phrase, "Just say no"? We know that in the heat of battle, or in the excitement of the moment, if we have prepared a response, or "approach" in this case, we can respond more favorably.

I have a friend who says, "When the burglar has already broken into your house, it's too late to run out to the garage and start lifting weights so you can overpower him. You have to prepare before he gets there."

SELL THE APPOINTMENT, NOT THE PRODUCT

I was teaching this at one church, and a fellow raised his hand and said, "How is it going to help our community if he joins our church?"

Good question. Very revealing question, too. It tells a lot about his view of the church's responsibility to the community, doesn't it? Would anyone deny that a vibrant church is an asset to a community? I bet someone could preach a sermon on that question. I'll leave it there, though.

Is it clear to you that we are selling the appointment and not trying to sell the prospect on all that Christendom has to offer at this point? Sell the appointment, not the product.

Remember, your only purpose in the approach is to set the appointment. Your only purpose in the appointment is to sell the prospect on the idea of attending a worship service at your church. At the worship service, your only purpose is in getting him or her to commit to the claims of Christ. . . . Ah! But then there's more, much more. In His time.

(It is probably obvious to you that you can use Team Seven for evangelism, the mission field, campus ministries, a youth program for a local church, or for any other endeavor where you need to gather in a harvest. We cover some of these areas in our seminars on networking the kingdom. We have a way of using Team Seven in a revival that will cause an explosion of attendance. The theme of this writing is reclamation. You'll just have to attend the seminar. See the Appendix.)

HOW TO TREE A COON

Why use a professional approach? Let me answer that by asking you a question. Why does the minister extend the invitation after the sermon? Obvious, isn't it? He wants to explain the claims of Christ before asking anyone to respond.

Why does a realtor insist on going with the client to show him a home instead of just giving the client the address and letting him go by and make a windshield appraisal?

You understand that you do not have to do it this way. This is not for everyone. These are people skills. Some of your team members are going to say to you, "I just want to be totally honest and up front with my prospects. I want to tell them on the phone what it is I want to meet with them about. I just want to be me."

I say to those people, "If you just want to be you, why do you put on a nice dress, paint your face, brush your hair and teeth before you go to church? Why don't you just go in your old, ragged bathrobe, yellow teeth, and stringy hair? Isn't that more the real you than the one painted and dolled up?"

I don't mean to sound harsh. What I want us to understand is that we've got to shake off some of our old ways of thinking and doing things. What we have been doing is holy, but not necessarily the technique we used.

Frank is Shirley's husband. Shirley is my younger sister. Frank never went to college. He doesn't say much. But he knows how to tree a coon. He said, "Jay, when you go coon hunting, you've got to think like a coon, and you've got to go where a coon goes. You've got to take a trained dog that knows how a coon thinks and where a coon goes." I am attempting to teach you how to teach your team to go "coon hunting," spiritually.

Remember, this is a step from nothing to something for our future team members. Most staff members believe that most inactive church members never were true believers. If that's true, then if by our influence we can get them under the influence of the gospel, isn't it our responsibility to do so? What do you think?

If by using good people skills, we can move from thirty percent effectiveness to seventy percent, and if we don't, aren't we in effect telling forty percent $(70 - 30 = 40)$ of our network of prospects, "Stay outside the door"?

When we didn't know, we were blameless on this point. But now we do know. Remember, God has a way of using a trained mind. What was it the Lord of the Harvest said to the wise servant who had invested his master's talents wisely? "You did well with small things. So I will let you care for much greater things" (Matthew 25:21).

YOUR POSTURE AND SETTING APPOINTMENTS

Your posture will have a great deal to do with your setting appointments. Let me illustrate this. Why do you think that it would be easy for the quarterback of the Dallas Cowboys, or any other football team, to set an appointment? They have the posture. People want to get with them.

Why do you think it is easier for the staff to set appointments than for the members? They have the posture. You may not have the same posture in the community as the person with whom you are setting the appointment, but remember you are calling about kingdom business and are representing the King.

That thought is to make us confident, not pious. Now for goodness sake, don't tell the prospect that. Not yet, anyway. I recommend that you stay away from religious terms and tones while setting appointments. Remember, he probably still cusses.

TOCKTICK OR TICKTOCK

I've said that the words we use are important. Words are all we have. How we marshal these words is important.

I heard a story one time of two men who went to Africa to sell shoes. One came home broke, the other a millionaire.

"What happened?" the boss asked the broke salesman. "No one wears shoes in Africa," he replied.

The boss asked the rich salesman, "What happened?"

The rich salesman replied, "No one had any shoes."

You see, a couple of words and an expectant attitude made the difference between wealth and poverty. It's the difference in tocktick and ticktock, isn't it?

They're only words. In music, they are only notes. In the hands of one composer, the notes come out as "Chop Sticks," whereas in the hands of another, the same notes come out as a symphony. It's all in how we arrange them.

It might also make the difference between heaven and hell for one of our prospects. This isn't casual stuff, is it?

FEAR OF FAILURE

Whether you think you can or you think you can't—you are right.

—Henry Ford

The reason most people don't succeed in business is the fear of failure (F.O.F.). I don't know where that comes from. I imagine it is from the Devil; it certainly isn't from God.

Now you already know that I am not a preacher. But I want to try something with you. I don't know if this is proof to you that there is a Devil or not, but when you get ready to call your first prospect, go over to the phone and see if it doesn't weigh more. Now call a friend to talk about something else and see if it isn't back to its normal weight. How about that? It felt like it weighed a ton earlier, didn't it? Wonder why that is?

I didn't mean to insult your intelligence; I just wanted to illustrate the point that the phone weighs more for all of us when calling a prospect. We all get scared.

GOD PROVIDES THE INCREASE

The thing that should give us confidence, not arrogance, is that if we honestly go in His name, they are not rejecting us, if they do, but His message. Now this does not let us off the hook if we are lazy or unteachable. There is no one so sickening as an arrogant, religious know-it-all who takes no responsibility for his actions. He accepts the credit when things go his way, and blames God when they don't. Huh-oh. There I went to preaching again, didn't I?

I think you get my message. We should use the best techniques we know, and there is no prize for stupidity. If we send our brightest young people, who desire to become staff members, to college and sometimes on to seminary, is it asking too much for a team member to learn an effective approach? We sow; "God provides the increase." It's like a physician who applies the medicine, but God heals the wound.

I find it helpful to tell my team members that we should not take the rejection personally.

SECRET AGENTS?

I've had people say, "If God wants me to speak to someone, He will lay that person on my heart." Would anyone deny that?

The same person says, "I let my life be my testimony. I don't have to go around telling people what they ought to do. They can see by my life." Oh?

There was a fellow who became a Christian when he came home from working in a logging camp. The pastor alerted the young man about the importance of keeping his testimony when he was ready to go back into the logging camp as a new Christian. The young man said, "Oh, I'll be all right."

The next year when he came home, the pastor asked, "How did you do as a new Christian in the logging camp?"

The young man replied, "They never found out."

Secret agents. That's sort of a dangerous attitude, isn't it? A few years ago there was a TV show called "Secret Agent Man." But I never heard of God having a secret agent, did you?

THERE IS A TIME TO SPEAK UP AND A
TIME TO SHUT UP

Whether it is in the business community or in the church, there is a time to speak up and a time to shut up. Sometimes it's hard to know when, isn't it?

My best story of this is the one about the farmer and his wife who were working out in one of their fields. This was when crop dusting by airplanes was in its infancy.

This young pilot landed his biplane crop duster there in the field. The farmer, in his overalls with no shirt, and his wife in a print dress, were leaning on their hoe handles watching as the dust was flying everywhere.

The farmer asked, "What would you charge to take me and Ethel up in that airplane?"

The young pilot had just earned his wings. He thought he'd have some fun with them. He said, "I'll take you both for a ride and not charge you anything, if you won't say anything during the flight. But if you speak, you have to pay me."

They climbed in. The young pilot pulled every stunt he knew. He did rolls and loop-de-loos and stalls and all.

He pulled in and landed, and said to the farmer, "Well, you don't owe me anything. You're the first one I ever took up who never said anything when I did all those tricks."

"Yeah. I almost said something when Ethel fell out."

Sometimes there is a time to speak up, wouldn't you say?

EXPECT THE BEST

Even though we prepare to the best of our ability, it is smart to remember, "You can't say anything right enough for the wrong person and you can't say anything wrong enough for the right person." Let's not forget, "Some people are in God's doghouse."

When we get ready to make the call or speak to our prospect in person, we should expect the best. You see, there may have been a kingdom representative in front of us preparing the way.

Make the call, set the appointment, invite the person.

Step 6: Your Goal Is to Build a Team Seven Deep—Fast

Your goal is to put together a team of seven people as quickly as possible. "Why quickly?" If there is no urgency, tomorrow will steal the opportunity from you.

Step 7: Commitment—Two Lunches and Two Coffees a Week

Being a Team Seven leader does not require a major time commitment. But it does require a time commitment. It's possible to use your unproductive time for this. It is not necessary that you give up your evenings with your family.

WHY THE COFFEE SHOP MEETING?

Why the coffee shop? This is our workplace. A great deal of the world's day-to-day business is done at the coffee shop.

Most of Team Seven's work can be done as we go about our everyday routine. There was a time when if we wanted to visit someone about the church, we went to their home, often uninvited, and imposed on their family life as well as our own.

A meeting scheduled at a coffee shop is far less threatening and less intrusive. Prospects love it because they don't have to clean the house, or apologize for it because we dropped in unannounced.

WE MEET OUR PEOPLE WHERE THEY ARE

The coffee shop is designed for the businessperson and not necessarily for the professional clergy. The businessperson feels comfortable in the coffee shop. Most are not comfortable intruding on, or being intruded on, in a family home setting. The Coffee Shop Meeting keeps us out of contrived situations. This is our workplace.

The clergy feel comfortable in any setting, but this is designed to enable the church members to relate in their prospect's setting.

But far more important, our prospects are more comfortable in the coffee shop.

SPOUSE PRESSURE IS REMOVED AT
THE COFFEE SHOP

Here is an important observation from the business world that may not be that obvious to all church staff members. When I recruit a man to help me in my business, whom do you think he is the most afraid to fail in front of? I've heard these big tough 250-pound men say, "Buddy, I'm the head of my house. If I decide to join you in your part-time business, it'll be my decision. My wife won't care. She does what I tell her."

Then he'd put his sales kit in the trunk of his car, and three weeks later it would still be there because he was afraid to tell her.

Did you know that a man would rather fail in front of anyone than his wife? I imagine the wives feel the same way, too.

Of course you already knew that. I say, "I did, too." Then wonder why we went to the home and asked him to make a decision for Christ, the most important of all decisions, in front of his wife and children? Am I making any sense?

Of course he must profess his faith in front of his wife and children and the world, when the time comes. But at this point, he may not have any faith to profess. I'm just saying, "Let's cut him a little slack," and meet with him first privately at the coffee shop.

TEAM SEVEN LEADS THE CHURCH
MEMBERSHIP INTO THE MARKETPLACE

Some might say, "But the coffee shop is not very private." I say to those, "You haven't been to the coffee shop lately." I've seen monumental private business decisions made at the coffee shop. If earthly decisions can be made there, heavenly decisions can be, too.

You'll read about the coffee shop as a modern-day watering hole in chapter 10. Remember that Jesus was at the local "coffee shop," the well, in the center of the marketplace when He met the "woman at the well."

Am I saying, "Don't do home visitation?" Does that need an answer? I'm just saying you can talk to a person at a coffee shop, in his or her setting, also. And in most cases, it is more comfortable to the one being contacted.

The thought of talking to someone about God in the marketplace may be offensive to you. I don't mean to offend anyone. I heard someone say one time, "Sometimes we become so heavenly minded that we are no earthly 'count."

I know that as staff members, many times we handle holy things so much that they become commonplace. We sometimes become so "churchy" that we can't communicate with our parishioners from the marketplace.

That's why Team Seven is so powerful. It leads and co-
erces the church membership from inside church walls into
the marketplace.

With Team Seven, the church membership bursts onto the
marketplace like Superman coming out of a phone booth.

So let's do two lunches and two Coffee Shop Meetings a
week. Do not quit doing any home visitation you are currently doing. Remember that verse, "This you should have
done and not left the other undone." Okay, maybe I used
it out of context. I know you get my meaning though, don't
you?

Step 8: Have a Team Seven Potluck

As soon as you get your first team seven deep, have a potluck
at your house or one of their houses.

POTLUCK! WHY A POTLUCK?

You are probably saying, "Potluck! Why a potluck?" For all
the same reasons that we had a Coffee Shop Meeting. And
more. This is a technique I learned from a friend in California who, along with his wife, built a network empire using
potlucks.

The main reason for the potluck is so that your team can
get to know each other, and do some bonding.

The team members probably have never even met. This is
what you hope is the situation, because you know then that
you are really breaking out of the church's network. Number 1 may be the mechanic, who brought number 3, the
dentist. Number 2, a publisher, may have brought number
4, a plumber, and so on.

Another obvious advantage of the potluck is that a great
deal of bonding goes on there. The plumber says to the
dentist, "Am I on your team or are you on mine?" You then
have a happening!

You see, a potluck doesn't sound threatening to a new
team member. Another thing. You may have recruited a

woman whose husband has little or no interest in coming to church. But he'll come to your home to break bread with you.

If you ask a new person to come to your home for a Bible study, cell group, or prayer meeting, this may be threatening. These are religious labels. After you get them involved in the church, put them into a cell group or Bible study group.

My recommendation is that you use the potluck basically only socially, for getting acquainted and bonding. Let the pastor do the preaching at the church. I am only talking about your first couple of potlucks.

You can move your team on into home Bible study, prayer groups, and so forth after your second or third potluck.

When you have a potluck at your house, it is my recommendation that you use styrofoam cups and paper plates. That's duplicatable. If you get out your nicest china, your future team leaders may not be able to do that, so they won't have a potluck. The name of the game: keep it simple and duplicatable.

Remember, the potluck is a tool used to implement Team Seven to get our new friends from nothing to something. Or should I say Someone? At our best, we are an attempt to be, as the song says, a "Rope of Love" that ties our networks to the kingdom.

"A Rope of Love" by O. J. Bryson, used by permission.

We are like Hosea, who bought back his wife, Gomer, from the slavery auction block for a homer and a half of barley. We are God's purchasing agents to reclaim His own. Ours is a mission of reclamation.

Step 9: Become a Student of the Business

Do the best you can to be the kind of person that God will accept, and give yourself to him. Be a worker who is not ashamed of his work—a worker who uses the true teaching in the right way.

—2 Timothy 2:15

My best counsel is, if you are going to work with Team Seven, become a lifelong student of the concept. You can dabble and do a little. But why not learn a lot and do a lot? It is a new concept in an area of great importance where you can become an expert as quickly as anyone else.

Your basic foundation of information can be found in the books *Team Sponsoring* and *Networking the Kingdom.* To this point, there is no other writing on earth on the subject. If you thoroughly study and comprehend these materials, you will be headed in the direction of becoming a real "unashamed workman" or "unashamed workwoman" at networking the kingdom.

All you will need then is a little experience, and to let the clock run. You don't need to know everything to begin, but there is no premium on ignorance.

> So be as smart as snakes.
> But also be like doves and do nothing wrong.
> —Matthew 10:16

Step 10: Teach the Above

Step 10 is to teach the other nine steps to your new team members as you continue your networking the kingdom. We want you to clone yourself. This is how we break the twenty-four-hour time barrier.

When I first entered the network marketing field, the common comment was, "If you can merchandise and recruit, you can get rich in networking." After I was in it a little while, I began to ask, "Why am I not rich from merchandising and recruiting? Why are my friends, who are doing the same thing, not rich?"

It soon dawned upon me that there was an important element that was missing in the formula. Three little words, and yet how big, had been left out. "If you can merchandise and recruit and *teach your distributors* to merchandise and recruit. . . ."

I found an old tape by the co-founders of my company.

They were saying, "Teach your distributors to teach their distributors to merchandise and recruit." I thought I had discovered something new, but their teachings had merely been lost in the process of being passed down through the distributor force. It never got to me. That's why you must teach your team what I was taught: "If I didn't tell you, I assume you don't know."

You and I must take the responsibility of teaching and bonding with the recruits we bring onto our team. If we don't, there is going to be a big influx of newly churched members who are untrained. We can't recruit them and dump them on the staff.

The staff will do their part. But we are the "Rope of Love" that holds them until the staff can get them involved in the mainstream of the church's life. We will lose some of them anyway, but we need to be sure that we have done our part to see that they don't fall through the cracks.

Step 11 (Optional): Attend a Two-Day Seminar on Networking the Kingdom

This is optional. At some point, perhaps early in your training, you should attend our two-day Networking the Kingdom Seminar. This seminar will give you a six-months head start on developing your networking skills. If you can't attend a training seminar, order the "*Networking the Kingdom How To Video.*" (Consult the Appendix.)

At the seminar, we get into how to make an approach to someone, how to set an appointment for a Coffee Shop Meeting, how to pull names of potential team members out of your prospects, how to get a new team member started, what to do after you get your first Team of Seven, and so forth.

We do an actual Coffee Shop Meeting. You get hands-on-experience.

I understand that not all of your team members can attend, but the staff and new team leaders will benefit greatly from this.

We will not discuss theology, for we have people from all faiths who attend. We only discuss procedures and concepts. Find a motif you can use, and then write your own symphony.

Don't try to reinvent the wheel. Learn the concepts, and as long as you stay on the playing field, use your own creativity.

A DEMONSTRATION IS WORTH A THOUSAND WORDS

When you see an actual demonstration of the Coffee Shop Meeting, it will make a thousand questions go away.

I remember my first snow-ski trip. My mind raced with, how do you do this and how do you do that? I couldn't imagine how you got the boots on your skis. I couldn't imagine how the people who rented the boots could know what kind of skis to rent me or even if they would. How do you get on the chair lift? How do you get off? How do you get up if you fall? How do you get from the motel to the place where you ski? How do you get the skis on the bus? How do you stop once you start down the mountain? Who would know if you ran off a cliff?

Once I arrived at the ski resort, everything was already taken care of. All my questions had already been answered by the people who had planned the resort. Everything fell into place, and I could no longer remember when I didn't know how everything fit together.

I am still developing my skiing skills, but my anxieties about how everything fits together are no longer a concern.

Unless a few leaders from your church attend and teach the others, I am afraid you may be about networking the kingdom like I was about snow-skiing. A person might come to the seminar and not ever do anything. But it is a known fact that few ever do much without attending one. Use your best judgment.

If I can clone myself by teaching and training those who come to the seminar, they can go back and teach what I taught them to their organizations. Hopefully, some will become *Networking the Kingdom* facilitators.

As we talk, please keep in mind that I am a teacher and not a salesman. If I say something that offends you, you must tell me. If you don't tell me, I can't do better. If I offend you, you will not introduce me to your friends. Am I making any sense?

Let's be friends.

The Ten Steps to Networking the Kingdom

Step 1: Make a list of twenty names

Step 2: Get a pocket or purse calendar

Step 3: Read *Networking the Kingdom* and listen to your first six tapes

Step 4: Automatic shipment of a tape each month

Step 5: Learn an effective approach for setting an appointment

Step 6: Your goal is to build a team seven deep—fast

Step 7: Commitment—two lunches and two coffees a week

Step 8: Have a Team Seven potluck

Step 9: Become a student of the business

Step 10: Teach the above

9

Schedule Appointments, Not Prospects

The task of the leader is to get his people from where they are to where they have not been.

—Henry Kissinger

You understand that by giving you all my business building techniques, as I train you, I am also training my competitors in the business field, don't you? Don't tell them that this information is in here because this stuff works as well making money as it does fishing for men.

In fact, in most of the chapters, the word *business* could be substituted for the word *church* and the book could be published as a business book. The concepts are true whether in the church or in the business community.

The most profound statement I will make to you about networking is this: I schedule appointments and not prospects.

What is the first thing a new business recruit, or new team member at the church says to you, when you tell him you want to go with him to visit one of his prospects? Exactly.

"When I think of someone, I'll call you."

No sir. That's not the way it works. It won't work that way. Here's how we do it to guarantee success.

I say to Joe, the mechanic, "Joe, get out your calendar. Your time is going to be at 5:30 Thursday afternoon at the Holiday Inn Coffee Shop. I want you to be there with one of your prospects. Now, Joe, you can't control if your prospect shows up or not. But you can control if you show up. If your prospect doesn't come, we'll have a training session. Did you get that time down? Now I want you to call me back tomorrow and tell me who is coming with you and that you have set a definite appointment."

Do I care whom he brings? Absolutely not. I only care that he is there and has a prospect with him. I am working out of his network now. The church is penetrating the community. We're networking the kingdom.

"I thought it would be more profound than that," you say. Nope. "God takes the common things of life to confound the wise."

Unlocking Your Calendar and the Coffee Shop Blitz

Somewhere there is a map of how it can be done.
—Ben Stein

Here's the map. I am going to show you how to unlock your calendar. I am also going to show you, simultaneously, how we do the Coffee Shop Blitz. By the way, you can use either of these techniques in your revivals.

Let's say you have built one, two, or three teams seven deep. If you have built only one so far, when you build two and three use the rest of this.

Let's say you are going to only work on Saturdays for your Team Seven project. You could use any day, or any time during the week. But for the sake of simplicity, let's do it this way. Get a piece of paper or your calendar, and lay it out like this:

SATURDAY

10:00

11:00

12:00

1:00

2:00

3:00

4:00

5:00

Now you go to the names of your team members on your different teams, or legs:

```
                    pastor
                    you
        1                            1
                    mechanic
        2           dentist          2
        3           ex-preacher      3
        4           barmaid          4
        5           banker           5
        6           conductor        6
        7           attorney         7
```

Start with Leg I, number 1. You call up Leg I, number 1, and say to Joe, the mechanic, "Joe, we are going to be doing a Coffee Shop Blitz this weekend, and Saturday morning at 10:00 is going to be your time. I want you to be there with a prospect."

Joe, who is really turned on, says, "Great. I'll be there."

Write Joe's name down in the 10:00 spot.

Now call Leg I, number 2. Say to Don, the dentist, the same thing. He responds, "My son has a game that morning. How about the afternoon?"

You say, "Okay, Don, how's 3:00?"

Put Don, the dentist, down at the 3:00 slot.

Go on to Leg I, number 3, the ex-preacher. He says, "I'm not interested. I'll be out of town."

Leg I, number 4, Barbara the barmaid, says, "11:00? Sure, I'll be there with a friend."

Leg I, number 5, the banker, says, "Can't make it at noon. How about later?" You say, "5:00 okay?" "A little late, but I think I can handle it."

Are you beginning to see the power of the process of working through these networks?

Numbers 6 and 7 on Leg I are out of pocket.

Now go to Leg II. Leg II, number 1, "Sure, 12:00 is fine."

Leg II, number 2, takes your 1:00 slot.

Numbers 3 and 4 on Leg II are busy.

Leg II, number 5, takes 2:00.

The only slot you have left open is 4:00. So you leave it open in case the others run a little long, or any other reason you can think of to procrastinate filling that slot. You've done pretty well, by the way. Your Saturday calendar looks like this:

SATURDAY

10:00 Leg I, number 1: Joe, the mechanic

11:00 Leg I, number 4: Barbara, the barmaid

12:00 Leg II, number 1

 1:00 Leg II, number 2

 2:00 Leg II, number 5

 3:00 Don, the dentist

 4:00

 5:00 Banker

Let's see what has happened. You've broken into six new layers of networks for the kingdom. Team Seven is absolutely the only way you could ever have forced those

networks to come into your life. That is the power of Team
Seven and the Coffee Shop Blitz. And you have still only
used about half of your team. Use the other half next Saturday for another blitz. Some of them don't even know you
had one this Saturday.

What would it do to your Sunday morning service if you
had ten members, each doing a Coffee Shop Blitz in ten different coffee shops on one particular Saturday? Remember,
average family size is three. So, 6 invitations times 10 Team
Seven leaders equals 60×3 to a family = 180 new people for
one Saturday's work. Could you stand it? Would your spouse
shout, "Glory"? If your spouse is out there helping you at the
Coffee Shop Blitz, by the end of the day, you both may feel
like you just pulled a Mormon Cart from St. Louis to Salt
Lake City. But it may be the best tired you have felt in a long
time.

I've seen it happen this fast and faster in the business
world. What if God's people got ahold of it? Do you see how
few people it takes to "bust out" a brand new church? Right
out of the Coffee Shop. Who would have thought it?

Other Good Time Slots

Other than Saturday, let me mention some other good time
slots for doing a Coffee Shop Meeting. By the way, in
the French translation of *Team Sponsoring, Le Parrainage
D'Equipes,* the Coffee Shop is called "au snack-bar."

If you are the pastor, or another staff member, or if you
are a church member who desires to devote a lot more time
to networking the kingdom, here are some times we have
found effective.

Problem: You have the time to see the people because this
is all you do. Your people don't have time to see you because
they are at work. Also those at work, who are the team leaders, can't go see the prospects for the same reason.

Solution: Find enough time slots when you or your people
can see each other.

These are choice times:

1. Breakfast on the way to work.
2. Morning coffee break.
3. Lunch.
4. Afternoon coffee break.
5. 5:30—After work, on the way home.
6. 6:30—Since you are already there, do another.

That gives you six slots a day, five days a week, which equals to thirty slots a week and you don't even have to break stride. That happens as you go about your normal routine.

Call Reluctance

When I am asked to give a business-building seminar, at one of the very first sessions I clear the air with the two following comments. See if you don't agree.

1. Show me your calendar, and I'll show you why your business is, or isn't, at the level you want it to be.

2. Most salespersons fail for one reason.

a. Is it because they aren't trained? No. Most are highly trained.

b. Is it because they don't have a good product? No. Most have a good product.

c. Is it because they don't qualify their prospects? No. Most have good prospects.

d. Is it because they don't represent a good company? No. Most do.

e. Is it because they don't have good telephone skills? No. Most do.

f. Is it because they can't close the sale? No. Most can.

g. Is it because they can't recruit good talent? No. Most can.

Then what are they doing wrong? Nothing.

The problem is that they just aren't seeing enough people. Everything they are doing is good. They just aren't doing it enough times. They have call reluctance.

There is a critical mass of people who must be seen. The invitation to visit our church must be made enough times to make Team Seven work. Remember no plan will work if you don't. And some won't, even if you do.

If you adopt this in your church or organization, you will have the same problem: how to motivate your people and get them over the fear of failure, the bosom buddy of call reluctance. Somehow you will have to find a way to get them to turn off the TV, the great time thief and electric income reducer, and get them out the door, and into the coffee shops.

I have found no other phrase that beats the simple, "You can do it. I know you can do it. I believe in you."

No-Shows

Let's talk about no-shows. It is seldom that a person does not show up for a Coffee Shop Meeting. But it does happen occasionally. Make it clear to your team member that you expect him there even if his prospect calls up and cancels at the last minute. Tell him you will train him during this time. If your team member does not write down the appointment when you make it with him, he will not be there. He cannot remember it. Get him to let you see his calendar and watch him write it down.

How long do you wait before you declare it a "no-show"? Fifteen minutes. If your prospect is fifteen minutes late, he is not coming. *He is not coming.* At the university, a student is only required to wait ten minutes on a lowly instructor. When I was a full professor, with tenure, and as division chairman, my students were only required to wait fifteen minutes for me. They never had to, I might add. So stop fretting after fifteen minutes, and go to training, or go to the phone and help your new team member make a call and set a strong appointment.

You seldom have a no-show in a one on one, or two on one appointment at a coffee shop. However, if you call a person up and say, "Come over to my house for a meeting," he seldom comes. He thinks he won't be missed. But one on one, he'll be there if you have any credibility at all with him.

If your new member keeps showing up without his prospect, you know it is usually one of three things. He is either setting a soft appointment (not making it a definite time and place), he is using the wrong approach, or his credibility is questionable with the prospect.

You're fishing for men. "If the fish ain't bitin', change your bait." If you're going after a real big fish, put on some real good bait. A lot of the big fish have "spit out a lot of hooks" in their lifetime.

In my business, I pray for no-shows. That's the only time I get to eat, or train my distributors.

Sometimes we run out of courage or commitment, but with Team Seven, we never run out of prospects or appointments. Our new team members keep bringing them to us. They also keep bringing us larger and larger doses of belief in ourselves, and that causes us to have more courage and commitment.

Lead Generation

If you are starting a new church, or new organization, and if you don't have enough leads, go to the Chamber of Commerce, and buy their calendar of events, or better still, join the Chamber.

Find out when the boat show is, or the autorama, or the garden show. Go down to the autorama in work clothes, a jumpsuit or such, and go around until you find someone you feel comfortable with. Ask him if you can be on his work crew for the weekend.

Tell him you are a car salesman, minister, or staff member, and you want to get your hands dirty, and meet some new people. They'll love it. You'll get more leads than you and all your members can follow up on. You may hear a little cussin', but most of them'll say, "Excuse me, preacher; that just slipped out."

If you already have an organization or an existing church, lead generation is a moot point. You hardly need it at all. You get your leads from your recruits now.

A Ten-Minute Coffee Shop Meeting Can Take Three Hours

If you have to travel one and a half hours each way to get to the coffee shop, you can't go to too many different coffee shops. Therefore schedule all of your Coffee Shop Meetings at the same coffee shop for a given day. Otherwise, the travel time can negate your effectiveness.

If a particular person lives too far away, schedule a whole day of Coffee Shop Meetings near that person.

Even though we need less than ten minutes to present our story, we schedule an hour, so we have some unhurried time for bonding. When the prospect first gets there, he may not be all that receptive. But after you've talked a while, sometimes he doesn't want to leave. If the meeting had been in your home, you could hardly ask the prospect to leave. After you have given him or her all the time you have allotted for that appointment, that's when you excuse yourself and get up and go to another booth.

Don't stay too long with one prospect at the coffee shop. Remember what happened to Cinderella when she stayed too long.

What you do is excuse yourself. Tell him you have another appointment and move to another booth. Or let Joe, the mechanic, sit there and visit with him, while you go to meet with Barbara, the barmaid, and her prospect a few booths away.

It's best not to sit in the booth that adjoins your previous party's booth, if they have not left. You don't have enough privacy. But if Joe, the mechanic, has left, stay at the same booth. It's starting to feel like home now, anyway, and you already have that waitress trained.

What an Opportunity!

Teach your team members to be on the lookout at every opportunity to find new leads for their team. You will be surprised at how many opportunities present themselves if you are sensitive.

I have a friend who tells the story of a young Army lieutenant who was sitting beside a colonel on a train. The colonel had given the young lieutenant a hard time back at the base.

Across from them sat a very attractive girl about the lieutenant's age, beside her grandmother. The cross-looking grandmother would poke the young girl every time she gave the young lieutenant "the eye." The colonel would then turn and stare at the lieutenant sitting beside him.

About that time the train went through a tunnel. It was pitch black, and the only sounds heard were those of a kiss and a slap. Smack! Pow!

As they came out of the tunnel, the colonel was thinking, "That brash young lieutenant, kissing that girl. But why did she slap me?"

The grandmother thought, "The nerve of that young man. But at least she had the spunk to slap him."

The girl was thinking, "I sure liked that, but why did Grandmother slap him?"

The lieutenant was thinking, "What an opportunity. I got to kiss the girl *and* slap the old man."

Opportunities abound. Be sensitive. Be winsome. Be on the lookout for those who can and should be reclaimed.

If we all did the things we are capable of doing, we would literally astound ourselves.

—Thomas A. Edison

several of their distributors, I was shocked at the calls I was getting from them, asking me what time of the day was best to go to the coffee shop to bump into people. I remembered the story of the fellow painting the yellow line down the highway. I bet you did, too.

One night I was watching "The Tonight Show," and Johnny Carson said, "If you want to find . . . [he named the particular type of network distributor], go to the coffee shop, and they will find you."

Some important points to be made here.

POINT MADE: The Coffee Shop Meeting is for a set time with a set prospect.

POINT MADE: Don't become an embarrassment to the kingdom by just "dropping in" at the coffee shop. You're liable to bump into Johnny Carson or his agent, and they'll tell everyone.

POINT MADE: If you don't tell your team members exactly what I have taught you, they will teach their team members only what you taught them. Watch out, because:

Enough information not taught,
May get you on the Johnny Carson show by default.

What Happens at the Coffee Shop Meeting?
What Doesn't Happen at the Coffee Shop Meeting?

Let me talk you through this, just like I would if you and I were sitting here having a cup of coffee.

I know that there are a lot of church members who already have effective techniques of inviting people to church. So I hasten to say, regarding our Coffee Shop Meeting, that this is *a* way, not *the* way. If what you are already doing is working, keep doing it. Use what you can from my suggestions, and disregard the rest.

I usually tell my business recruits what I was taught, "Fail my way first." I give them all my best techniques, style, nuance, and verbiage, and they still go out and do it however they want to. You probably will, too. And your way will probably be as good as mine. But if you don't have a way, try mine.

What Not to Do at the Coffee Shop Meeting

It is my recommendation that this meeting only be a point of contact, a touch point if you please. You should invite them to attend our worship service, and not make a confrontational evangelistic experience out of it. That's my recommendation. (But if you feel that you should get up on top of a table, lead them in prayer and a few choruses, preach them a sermon, and then give an invitation, go right ahead. But that's not my recommendation.)

Use all the people skills, fellowshipping skills, and bonding skills you have. I just suggest that you leave church cliches back at the church. Try to remember how you used to talk to a neighbor. (I don't mean cussing.)

This doesn't seem to be the time to get out your Bible, and take Joe's prospect down the Roman Road to Salvation there in front of his banker, attorney, bartender, and ex-girlfriend, who may be sitting in the adjoining booth. (But if you want to get out your Bible and take your prospect down the Roman Road to Salvation, go right ahead. I just recommend that you do it in another location at another time. Use your own judgment.)

His banker, attorney, bartender, and ex-girlfriend, may not be there in the next booth, but if you get too churchy, Joe and his prospect will both imagine that they are, and worse. Use some common sense. You're going to do it how you want to, anyway. I just make these suggestions. Again, I don't care if you get up and deliver a sermon, but Joe and his prospect may. This is their turf. Let's talk their language.

The Coffee Shop Setting

Let me set the scene at the coffee shop for you. At our seminars, the most requested item is the actual live Coffee Shop Meeting. Once you see one, it all seems so logical. Until you see one, I'll try to draw you a verbal picture.

Here it is. I have arrived early and told the waitress, "I prefer a booth or table in the back, a corner, or to the side, because we are going to be talking privately. Once you bring our coffee, we'd rather not be disturbed until we are through. We won't think you are neglecting us, and we are big tippers, too."

Be generous with your tips. If you are going to be going there often, you want the waitress to be glad to see you. If the owner pays for the air conditioning, the heat, and the rent for your office away from the office, you are getting off light.

I go ahead and locate the booth or table, and put my things down there. Then I usually go back out to the lobby and wait for Joe, the mechanic, my new team member, who is bringing a friend with him.

If Joe has been with me before, I will wait at the booth, because the introductions are more private and intimate. The chances are I have never met his friend.

Either I have called the friend and invited him for my new team member, Joe, the mechanic, or preferably, Joe called and set the appointment. Either way, the prospect was told that I was going to be with Joe. I don't like surprises, and his prospect doesn't either. If he hadn't told him I was going to be there, the prospect would probably have felt that he had been set up.

Joe, the mechanic, used (or I used) the recommended approach that is written out in chapter 8, "Ten Steps to Networking the Kingdom," or we made up another that was more comfortable to us. I call it an approach to the prospect, in order not to confuse it with an invitation to visit our Sunday morning worship service. Anyway the prospect is here now to talk with us.

Sometimes You Have to Think Fast

I usually do not know whom my new team member is bringing; I don't care. It makes no difference to me. I just want him to bring someone. But when this is the case, sometimes you have to think fast. Every situation is different, and sometimes it can get downright comical.

A pilot friend from Florida who is with Delta Airlines told me a story that illustrates this point.

This New Yorker was small in stature and had not flown much, so he already had a queasy stomach. He was assigned a window seat. When he got to his seat, there was a great big Texas cowboy asleep in the aisle seat, with his hat pulled down over his eyes, and his long legs stretched out in the aisle.

The New Yorker had to awaken him in order to get into his window seat. The cowboy was half asleep as he grumbled and let him in.

The plane took off, the cowboy went back to sleep, and the New Yorker got sick. As he sat there, wanting to get out, he didn't want to awaken the cowboy again, but he was about to lose it as he fidgeted with his seat belt.

Finally, he could stand it no longer. He stood up and took a step over the cowboy. Just as he got straddled halfway across, he lost it all, right in the cowboy's lap.

He sat back down real fast, and looked over at the cowboy who was now awake, and said to the cowboy, "Do you feel better now?"

Sometimes you have to think fast. Have fun with your prospects, and be real. They'll like that, and you.

Introduce Your Prospect to the Team Leader (Me)

This time I am waiting at the booth. We greet each other and sit down. Joe, the mechanic, has brought Don, the dentist, with him, and he introduces him to me. What does he say? What he says is not that important. What is important, is that he transfer his trust of me, his friend, to Don, the dentist.

How does he accomplish this? First of all, he doesn't need to go into a glowing report of how wonderful I am, and all my accomplishments and my genealogy.

He simply says, "Don, this is my friend, Bill. He is a teacher. We go to the same church and met at a potluck one night. My wife and I have gotten to know and like him, and I wanted you to get to know him, too. I thought you would hit it off. Bill, he's all yours."

That assumes that my name is Bill, which it isn't. But that is about all there is to the introduction. From here on out, Joe, the mechanic, says very little unless I ask him something. He watches and learns.

Goal: Sell Him on Visiting Our Sunday Morning Service

I only have one mission in mind at this time. Now, we all know what the end result of my mission is. But at this time I am not going to lay all that on him.

My one and only goal of this Coffee Shop Meeting is to invite him, and to sell him on attending our Sunday morning worship service, and to get him to say yes.

How am I going to do that? Shouldn't I tell him about our pastor, the fellowship of the people, the warmth, the music program, the program for young people, the children's programs, the way we are growing, and how the Lord is blessing our church? Yes. But I am not going to use puffery or try to oversell our church. I just want him to know that our staff and church care about individuals and how our church relates to our community.

It is not important that we convince him that our pastor can leap tall or small buildings. What we want him to know is that our pastor is an effective communicator and that he cares.

Okay, let's do it.

One of the first things I am going to say to Don, the

dentist, is this. "Don, I am not a salesman, I am a teacher. But I have something I wanted to run by you. I don't know if you will be interested or not, but all I want to do is to get you to promise me you won't say 'No' the first time I tell you about it. I don't care how long it is until you say, 'Yes.' Is that fair enough?"

After we chitchat for a minute or so, I then say something like this, "Don, we have some fantastic things going on at our church, etc., etc."

Then I proceed to tell him whatever is important about our church. But at a point, fairly early, the following question must be asked:

"Don, we were wondering, are you and your wife going to church anywhere, regularly now?" I put the word "regularly" in there to soften the question, and to give him a way out to protect his dignity. Don, like most people, would not want to say out loud to a stranger, and that's what I am to him, that he never attends church.

That way, he can respond with his dignity intact, "Well, no, we're not attending anywhere, regularly."

You understand that I am only talking about people who used to go to church and who now do not. If you know the person is lost, or if you find out that he is lost at the Coffee Shop Meeting, get him or her in touch with a staff member, or someone skilled in soul-winning. We are only talking in this book about how to reach that mass of people who are currently unchurched but used to be churched. There are thousands of books that will teach you soul-winning, but this is the only one I know about on reclamation.

Body English

Now this is not the time to "pounce" on him. I recommend that you sort of "lay back in the woods" a little. Lower the pitch of your voice, and speak a little softer and slower. Lean back in your chair, like a friend would. Don't jump halfway over the table on your elbows, as if to say, "I got me a trophy."

My sponsor taught me something about body English. Let me talk with you a little about it. See if you don't agree.

Have you ever been in a small room with a group or in a hot tub with a bunch of snow skiers, after a hard day on the slopes? The hot tub is outside in the snow. Sometimes the person who has the smallest network and the smallest business is the loudest one. If anyone brings up a subject, he wrests it away and begins to expound from the center of the tub. Sometimes it's hard to visit with others. Sometimes it's good to just be cool.

My sponsor told me, "When you are standing and talking with someone, lean back a little, and talk a little softer. They will lean a little toward you. Lean in toward them, and talk a little louder, and they take a step backwards."

I've tried it hundreds of times. People react as if on cue. Have you ever noticed that the most effective ministers, when ready to make a significant point, lower their voice almost to a whisper, as we lean in to catch it? The less effective reach a significant point and yell it at us.

How 'bout that?

God doesn't come in the whirlwind. He speaks "with a still, small voice."

This is probably the time when Don, the dentist, is going to tell us why he isn't going to church. This is the time to listen and let him talk. The reasons people don't attend are as varied as the snowflakes, and as numerous as the sands in the ocean.

Don't act shocked. He may say, "I was active in the church once. I was a deacon in that other town. But one day I was pulling this kid's tooth, and his mother came in and cussed me out. Her husband was the chairman of the deacons. I've never set foot back inside a church."

No matter what he says, be sensitive. But go on with your goal, which is to get him to attend the worship service this coming Sunday at your church, or the first Sunday he has free.

Get a Commitment to Attend This Sunday

"Don, I'd like for you and Linda and your children to think about visiting our church sometime. In fact, I'd like for you to be my and Joe's guest, this coming Sunday morning for the late worship service. That's the one that starts at 10:30."

I didn't invite Don to Sunday School this Sunday, because I wanted to be there to greet him and to show him around. Since I am older than he is, we wouldn't be in the same class.

I say, "I could meet you at the main entrance, the south entrance off of Memphis Street at about 10:15. I'll introduce you around to some of my and Joe's friends."

If Don says, "I'll try to be there," what is he saying? You're right. He's not coming. *He is not coming.* How do you get him to give you a definite commitment? The mind is the laziest organ in the body, and will take the path of least resistance. So help him make the decision.

Say something like this, "Don, Joe's wife is planning for you and me to go out to eat with them Sunday. Now if you can't come this Sunday, that's okay. But I need to know, 'cause if Joe and I tell her you and your family are coming, and we don't show up with you, she'll kill us."

"If you can't come, that's okay, but we've got to tell her something."

The Close

You can tell I am a teacher and not a salesman. Zig Ziglar says, "If you don't close, all you have done is told a good story." Getting a definite commitment to be there Sunday morning is the close.

Someone might say, "I don't like tension. I couldn't be that strong." Be as strong as you can. Remember, there was plenty of tension at the cross.

It's easy to score thirty-six points in Texas Stadium in Dallas, Texas, on Wednesday afternoon, when you are the only one on the field. But this Coffee Shop Meeting is

the equivalent of Monday Night Football, and the Redskins
are lined up across the scrimmage line, and they don't want
us to score.

My Redskins friends may not like the comparison of the
Devil and God's team lined up that way, but you get my
point.

Of course, you should be as sensitive with your Team
Seven prospects as you would be with your traditional prospects. Even in traditional visitation, you still have to "ask
for the order."

Follow-Up Packs

In the old general store, often someone would come into the
store to buy something, and didn't. As they left, they often
said, "Got to think about it, but I'll be back."

The proprietor often responded in jest, "Let me hold your
watch, then."

The follow-up pack that I recommend uses that concept
in reverse. We let them "hold our watch." We let them take
something of value with them. "Why?" Of course.

It gives us a reason to get back with them face to face.
Have your team leaders and team members pay for their own
follow-up packs, which they use, and they won't lose them.
They will remember where they left them. When I pay for
them, they can't even remember to whom they loaned them.

If Don gives me a reason why he can't attend this Sunday,
or isn't sure he even wants to visit our church, I say this
to Don:

"Don, we don't care when you and Linda decide to say
yes. We're in no hurry about that. Joe and I just don't want
you to say no today.

"Our goal is not to get you to say yes today. If you say,
'No, I'm not ready to decide right now. I want to think about
it,' that's okay.

"Here is our goal. As we walk out the front door of this
coffee shop, we want you to be saying to yourself, 'I may not
be ready to decide about a church right now, but when I am,

I'd like to go to church with them. I like the way they treated me.' That's our goal. Fair enough?"

After I listen, then I say, "Don, Joe and I have a packet that we would like for you to take home with you. You and your wife look it over. It has a tape from our pastor. It's short. On one side, the pastor describes our church and tells you a little bit about what we have to offer, and his feeling as to where the church is going, and maybe how you could fit in. The back side of the tape has about ten minutes from one of his better sermons. I think it's his sugar stick. We don't tell everyone that he's the best preacher in town. We just say, 'There's not anyone any better.'"

We also put a church bulletin, a map of how to get there, and another pamphlet about one of our other programs. (If you have a Saturday Nights in Los Angeles or a Fourth Dimension outreach program, or any other special piece of literature, put it in the packet. No more than one tape and three pieces of literature.) "Don, we need to get our follow-up pack back from you in a few days, so we can hand it to someone else." I gave him the packet so I would have a reason to get back with him face to face. I made this last statement to him so he would know it had value to me, and so he wouldn't throw it away. It's like a string tied around his finger. It keeps reminding him.

Handling Objections

There is a difference between an excuse and an objection. An excuse is what your team member gives you for not setting the coffee shop appointment. An objection is what a prospective member gives you.

I tell my associates we could print the objections out on a card and hand them to the prospect, and say, "Just check off the one you want to use." They all give the same ones.

In your kingdom networking, the same is true. My Sunday School class president shared this with us, so now I share it with you. I think it illustrates the point very effectively.

It seems this minister was tired of people giving him the

same excuses for not attending church. He discovered one day that there were a lot of words he could substitute for *church* to better illustrate the foolishness of the excuses. Here are a few examples of his substitutions of the word "wash":

1. I was made to "wash" as a child.

2. People who "wash" are hypocrites—they think they are cleaner than other people.

3. There are so many different kinds of "soap," I could never decide which one was right.

4. I used to "wash," but it got so boring I stopped.

5. I still "wash" on special occasions, like Christmas and Easter.

6. None of my friends "wash."

7. I'm still young—when I'm older and have gotten a bit dirtier, I might start "washing."

8. People who make "soap" are only after your money.

—Rev. Sidney Lang, Dublin, Ireland

Some Plant: Others Water

When I offer a customer a product or try to recruit a distributor, I am seldom affected emotionally by whether that person says yes or not. "Why? Is it because I don't care?" No. That's not it at all.

When I began in my business, I made a commitment. I decided that it did not matter to me who did and who didn't join me. I was going to do it. I knew that if I called on enough customers and saw enough potential recruits, I would be successful. Now, when I make a presentation and the person says no, I get back in my car and just yell, "Next!" I learned that from a Crown Direct in California. Then I put them on my "I'll get you yet list." Crown Direct is a title for someone with a very large network.

If you are not in the people business, get into the people business because that's where it's happening. If you are on a church staff, you are in the people business. If you are in the people business, that's about the only attitude you can have and keep your sanity. Everybody can't harvest. Some have to plant, and some have to water. I am not a preacher. So if I don't get my applications just right, be patient with me. But Paul said:

> I planted the seed of the teaching in you, and Apollos watered it. But God is the One who made the seed grow.
> —1 Corinthians 3:6

There is another verse of Scripture, but we have to be careful not to be too hasty in its application. That's the one that tells us what to do when we've done our best to be a witness:

> If any town refuses to accept you or its people refuse to listen to you, then leave that town. Shake its dust off your feet. This will be a warning to them.
> —Mark 6:11

Some People Are in God's Doghouse

There is another thing that I don't understand, but I accept it. I can present the same business plan or invitation to church at the coffee shop to one prospect, and he jumps up and down and yells, "I'll do it!" I present the same thing to another and he looks at me and says, "Whom do you think you are kidding?" Wonder why that is? Sometimes the timing isn't right for them.

I've heard preachers say that about their sermons, too. One church will have a revival, and the same sermon will cause another church to split. Wonder why that is? Jim Roan says, "Some people are in God's doghouse and we might as well leave them alone."

What I am saying is I don't think God expects us to become a professional objection handler. I think he expects us to use common sense and be patient. Just know when objections come up, you were not the first. Be loving, be caring, be winsome, be Christ-like, and you'll do all right.

Why People Buy from You

I heard a friend of mine, who is a salesman, say one time, "There's one basic reason why people buy from you and not your competitor."

What would you think it is? Let's see.

1. You give good service? Nope. Most give good service.

2. You have good packaging? Nope. Most have good packaging.

3. You have good products? Nope. Most have good products.

4. You made a good appointment? Nope. Most do.

5. Your company gives a good guarantee? Nope. Most do.

6. Your company has a good reputation? Nope. Many do.

7. You are trained. Nope. Most are.

8. The person buying the products likes you? Yes!

The fact that the person actually likes you has more to do with his purchasing your product than any other reason. Of course, he won't continue to purchase from you if you don't have the other seven things. But the initial sale goes to the person he likes.

Now, I have to be careful with carrying this illustration too far in networking the kingdom. But at the initial Coffee Shop Meeting, it is important that we begin bonding and establishing a relationship with the prospect. God has no hands but our hands. We are His hands at this point. It is important that the prospect likes us. We are His only touch point.

What If He Joins Another Church?

I was teaching this concept at a church, and we were having a meeting where we reported back on our progress or lack of it. One man got up and said, "I caught one, but he got away. I told him why he should bring his family and get back in church, and he went off and joined another church."

The brother was really disappointed. I said, "Sir, that's networking the kingdom, too."

I was helping as the choir director at a church one time, and we had purchased a new organ. I had made arrangements for the church organist to give lessons to one of our young people.

The pastor, who was usually pretty open to most things, came in and said, "No."

I said, "But pastor, this young lady could someday become our organist."

"Nah. We'd probably just get her trained, and then she'd go off to some other church."

I wish I had thought to say, "We'd be networking the kingdom, then." But I didn't. I dropped the subject. Besides, that was a long time ago.

Sometimes I think we do get our minds so fixed on our own local ministry that we come to look on other churches as competitors. Not often. But we need to be careful at that point.

The Mobile Coffee Shop Meeting

We can use the Coffee Shop Meeting anywhere. If I meet a person on an airplane, and I tell him of our efforts at networking the kingdom, and he gets excited about it, I need a place to plug him in. If I live in Kansas City, and he lives in Nashville, neither my church nor I can be of much personal help to him unless we have one of our own team leaders

located there. So I loan or sell him a book and six tapes and
say, "If you'll give me your card, I'll have one of my pastor
friends' team leaders contact you."

When I get home, I look on my Automatic Shipment
Program list and find out who is networking the kingdom. I
then have my secretary send a note to that church, pastor,
priest, or Sunday School teacher. Then I say, "You owe me
one." What a concept!

I also request a follow-up report that the person was or
was not contacted. If he wasn't, I send the name to someone
else. There is no responsibility without accountability. What
is so great about that is that you can do that as well as I can.

Every church or team leader has their network as near to
them as their phone, just as my network is to my phone.

Can you imagine how happy that would make Jesus? All
these business men and women reaching across the aisles of
a plane and saying, "Hello, my name is Jim. What's yours?"

The person across the aisle asks, "What do you do?"

You say, "I'm a physician by profession. But what I am
really excited about is the technique our church is learning
called networking the kingdom.'"

He says, "Yeah. How does that work?" Or else, he turns
toward the window and goes to sleep. Either way, you have
networked the kingdom.

11

The Rule of Seven

The Rule of Seven: When a church member has seven close friends in a church, he or she will never leave it.

Remember the Rule of Seven: "When a church member has seven close friends in a church, he or she will never leave it." How strong, how strong, especially if he brought the seven to the church. If that rule is true, and it is, what is your goal once you get Don, the dentist, to the Sunday morning worship service? Exactly! You want him to make seven new acquaintances. "How do I do that?" Take him around with you and keep saying to your friends: "I have someone I want you to meet."

When Don goes with you to church Sunday morning, the only phrase you need to remember is this: "Pastor, do you have a minute? *I have someone I want you to meet. This is Don, the dentist. Joe, the mechanic, introduced us.*"

Take Don around and say that to each one you introduce him to. Let him know that you want him to know your friends. Don't stay long with anyone. Don't give a seminar, or let anyone else give one. Keep him moving through your network. Make sure Don and his wife meet at least seven new people at the church. He'll feel that it is his church before he leaves.

If you don't teach your team members to duplicate this process, some will let the "parade go by," while they stand there with their "trophy," and a blank expression on their faces, like a calf looking at a new gate. Remember:

Greet the friends by name.
> —3 John 1:14 (King James Version)

The End Result: He Joined the Church

Don, the dentist, came with us to our Sunday morning worship service and, after a few Sundays, joined our church.

Team Seven has completed its primary job, which was to seek out and reclaim someone for the kingdom. Don's team leader continues to include him on his team activities such as potlucks, and gets him involved in networking the kingdom. For Team Seven training, the team leader gives him a copy of *Networking the Kingdom* and his first six tapes. (Let Don, the dentist, pay for his own copy and tapes.)

But at this point, the church treats Don, the dentist, exactly like any other new member. Just plug him into the regular church activities. Give him the same new member training you give anyone else. Don't change one thing.

Since our first goal is to reclaim former church members and lead them to church membership at our church, including all that this means for our church, then I think you can see the beginning of some wonderful new challenges.

A Good Problem

When I first developed the Team Sponsoring concept for the business world, the biggest criticism we received was, "I am sponsoring people so fast, I don't have time to train them, and no one is selling any products."

My reply was, "How much were they selling before you

sponsored them? They aren't authorized to sell until you recruit them. They don't know how to sell until you train them. If you recruit faster, you have to train faster." Good problem. Can you take the application from there?

The fact remains that you *can* bring too many people into your business at a time—unless you have a training program that is equal to your recruiting program.

The same is true of the church. You can grow too fast, if you aren't handling the paperwork, if you aren't plugging these new people into your existing programs at the church.

Again, don't start any new programs. But you must let the new people know of the old programs because they are new to them. My best recommendation is to plug them into Sunday School, or Bible study if that's what you call it. If you get the new folks into the old stuff, you've got it made. Assume they know nothing until you personally tell them.

Bring the Congregation Along

Although you don't toss Team Seven out to the congregation from the pulpit, at some point you are going to have to tell them why all these new people are joining their church, and why that new fellow got "their seat."

You will have growing pains. Most of the congregation will thrill at the excitement, but watch out. Some people won't understand why they had to park two blocks from the church.

Most of God's people will "go with you to the wall," but if someone has a hidden agenda, he can take it out on you, and blame it on his lawn mower. One reason is as good as another.

Some will ask, "But why do people have to become church members in order to be on my team?" Answer: We're reclaiming them for the Lord, not just putting them on a team. When they have joined the church, in all that this means, we have brought them back into the fold. If you don't anchor them to the church, you run the danger experienced in the Jesus Movement of the 1960s. A lot of wonderful things happened, but much fell through the cracks.

Please don't let Team Seven become in your mind an argument over church membership when there are those away from the fold, hurting and lonely. Once we get them back, we can teach them everything we want them to know.

Don't try to draw me into what is required and not required for church membership. I gladly concede that you would win that debate with me, for I am no theologian. But I am an expert in recruiting talent and reclamation. Debate with me on those issues, and I might be a more formidable challenge. I know what membership requirements are at my church. You know what they are at your church. But don't misquote me on the matter of church membership, because I did not discuss it. If you don't know the requirements at your church, ask your pastor.

If the church's goal is to at least double in membership in twelve months (and it certainly should be), when we reach our goal, half of the membership may not have a history of tithing, studying the Bible, bonding, etc.

My best thoughts at this time would be to introduce them to your Sunday Bible study or Sunday School, whatever you call it, as soon as you can. Maybe even before they join the church. But their first visit should be to the worship service. They can feel anonymous there.

If we invite them to Sunday School or Bible study before they get acclimated to the church, they may not come for fear we will call on them to pray or read. They may not be able to read. But at the worship service they can hide out.

We as church leaders handle holy things so often that sometimes we forget that other people stand in awe of the church. They sometimes feel awkward there.

Hillbilly Preachers and Chants

This was brought home to me very vividly recently. As I told you earlier, I was raised in the foothills of the Great Smoky

Mountains. Over there, a preacher wasn't considered to be much of a preacher unless he had taken off his coat, rolled up his shirt sleeves, loosened his tie, and was walking on two inches of his britches cuffs, and could hardly talk above a whisper by the end of the sermon.

Understanding this, a longtime friend of mine, a soloist for the Temple Emmanuel Synagogue, recently invited me to one of their Friday evening services.

I was curious about hearing him do this, because when I had first met him, years ago, he was playing the washtub for the "Booger Boys." That was their comedy name. Actually they were the quartet for a weekly religious hour show on national radio. He now has a Ph.D. in music from North Texas State University.

I'd never been to a Jewish service. I went. You know what? I didn't know when to stand up and when to sit down. I was constantly concerned that people were watching me. I knew that everyone there knew and cared that I didn't know which book to sing out of, or even if I was supposed to sing, or if I was supposed to chant.

Now folks, I've been to a lot of churches. I felt welcome but uncomfortable. Not with the people, but with the unfamiliarity of the service.

Let's at least acknowledge that our guests on Sunday may feel some of that.

Meet Them at the Door

I would rather be a doorkeeper in the Temple of my God.
—Psalm 84:10

There are those in life who stand by doors and open them for other people. There are those in life who open financial doors, and other doors of opportunity. But if in our lives, we can just stand by the door of the house of the Lord and introduce people to the warmth of His love, we will have filled a gap that often goes unnoticed.

As our friends are being reclaimed, someone needs to meet them at the door and introduce them around to seven new friends.

> I stand by the door.
> I neither go too far in, nor stay too far out,
> The door is the most important door in the world—
> It is the door through which men walk when they find
>   God.
> There's no use my going way inside, and staying there,
> When so many are still outside and they, as much as I,
> Crave to know where the door is.
> And all that so many ever find
> Is only the wall where a door ought to be.
> They creep along the wall like blind men,
> With outstretched, groping hands.
> Feeling for a door, knowing there must be a door,
> Yet they never find it . . .
> So I stand by the door.
> The most tremendous thing in the world
> Is for men to find that door—the door to God.
> The most important thing any man can do
> Is to take hold of one of those blind, groping hands,
> And put it on the latch—the latch that only clicks
> And opens to the man's own touch. . . .
> So I stand by the door.[1]

Wow! So well said. It is *so* comfortable way inside the church. But it is *so* scary from the outside. If we can't always be at the door, let's at least be there on the Sunday when our prospects do come to greet them and introduce them around to our friends. Remember, ours is a mission of reclamation, a step from nothing to something. A step from the cold into the warmth, if you please.

Many churches have a new member class that lasts four Sundays. One Sunday the priest or minister teaches it. The next week it is taught by the education director, the next by the minister of music, and the last by the youth director—or some such arrangement. This is an effective way to get the basic information to the new members.

Summary: We recommend no new programs or staff. Plug your new team members into the current program of activities. Do look out for a parking lot or two, close by. The church may want to take an option on a couple of lots, just in case.

And most of all, let's look for the sheep that lost its way. Let's reclaim it for Him. We can do a lot with a person once we have him or her back under the Shepherd's care. It's an old song. But what a message for the moment from Elizabeth Clephane:

> "Lord, Thou hast here Thy ninety and nine;
> Are they not enough for Thee?"
> But the Shepherd made answer:
> "This of Mine has wandered away from Me;
> And although the road be rough and steep,
> I go to the desert to find My sheep,
> I go to the desert to find My sheep."[2]

12
Transferring Leadership: The Weaning Process

Help thy brother's boat across, and lo!
thine own has reached the shore.
—Old Proverb

Every team leader was helped to get to the level of team leader. You didn't inherit the position. You earned it, but you had a lot of help. Someone said, "If you ever see a frog sitting on a fence post, you can bet he didn't get there by himself."

The purpose of this chapter is to teach you how to put a frog on a fence post.

At some point, you have to transfer leadership. Otherwise, you can't clone yourself. How do you know when a person is ready to have the leadership transferred to him, and at what point do you do it?

Our children grow up and go out on their own, but they are always our children. Your people who grow up and become team leaders, even when they break away from you, are still in your group.

I was snow skiing in Snowmass, Colorado, with an orthodontist and his wife from Canada. He said, "When we explain your Team Seven concept to someone in our network, we say, 'We've got a bus. We're putting people on the bus, usually seven. By the time we get seven on the bus, usually one of the seven becomes the bus driver. When we find the bus driver, we let him drive. We go load up another bus. But we never get too far from the first bus driver, because he might run out of gas.'"

Sometimes transferring leadership is called the weaning process. There is nothing as unnatural as a three-year-old calf still suckling on its mamma. Imagine holding a bird inside our fist. If we hold it too close, we smother it. If we just keep holding it, even if we don't smother it, it begins pecking, wanting out.

Rule: *Never Do for a Team Member What He Can Do for Himself.*

The cardinal rule, from the day a team member joins your team, is, "Never do anything for a new team member that he can do for himself." Begin weaning from the first day. At some point, the new team member is expected to stand on his own two feet. This is that point.

Always Go Where the Information Is

Remember, as your network grows, it is doomed for failure unless you get all the information you were taught to everyone in your network. The best way to do this is to hand them a copy of *Networking the Kingdom* and the six tapes.

This information is to give them direction. If they don't have that information, they become like a scene I saw on the Monty Python Flying Circus. They had a "race for the people with no sense of direction." You can imagine the rest.

If you don't know where you are going, it doesn't matter how fast you travel. How do you know when you get there if you don't know where you are going? Why force our team members to chart their own course?

My son Scott and I were invited to go on a barefoot cruise down through the Abaco Cays (called keys), in the Bahamas, on the C.L.S. *Dreamer,* a large sailing yacht owned by one of my upline leaders. We chartered another yacht, also; there were six adults and six college students.

We had been sailing for about three or four days. Each evening we would dock and take the dinghy over to the shore and sit and applaud God's sunset.

One evening, after dinner, we were sitting around under the stars singing and enjoying God's beauty. Someone said, "Wonder what those back home who said, 'No' to our offers to them to join us in our networking business are doing tonight?"

About that time one of the college students spoke up and brashly challenged the adults to a race the next day to the next port. The students would take one yacht and the adults the other.

I thought it was a joke because the two adults in charge of the yachts were seasoned sailors. But the young people goaded us into the race. I thought: "Piece of cake."

The next morning we left port at the same time. Same wind, same size yacht, same everything, except we had the experience.

As we pulled out, the college students were cheering like crazy and began chanting, "Follow us, follow us," as one of the students held up the navigation charts. A "whipped pup" look went over all of us as someone ran downstairs to check on our charts. Sure enough, the students had our navigation charts. Both groups knew the harbor of our destination, but the charts told us how to get there.

No contest. The rest of the day we were relegated to following those with superior information. How did we feel? Like those in the "race for the people with no sense of direction."

POINT MADE: The newest sailor can reach harbor before the most seasoned sailor if he has the charts and the other doesn't. The newest team member can build his team faster than the staff member if he or she has the book and tapes and the staff member doesn't.

POINT MADE: Go with the boat that has the information. Work in your teams that are getting your Team Seven charts down through the organization: *Networking the Kingdom* and the six tapes. Those without the charts may know the destination, but they do not know how to get there.

POINT MADE: Always work in your teams where the information is. The other teams just tag along, trying to chart their own course, often crashing on the rocks of "lost interest," "This won't work," "Yeah but . . . ," "If only . . . ," or "This is the staff's job."

POINT MADE: The ship that is in front is not always ahead in the race. The one with the navigation charts knows when to make his tack to catch the most favorable wind to reach harbor. With Team Seven, some may just be doing a bunch of first-level networking which results in simple pew packing. If the team is using its charts, *Networking the Kingdom* and the six tapes correctly, the pews are packed permanently. "We can't direct the wind, but we can adjust the sail."

By the way, I heard a surefire cure for seasickness: Sit under a tree.

Look for a Booker

One master teacher of network marketing says, "When I find a booker, I know I can get out of a leg, and start a new one." A booker is someone who can take his own prospects, or pull the names out of his new associates, and book the Coffee Shop Meeting, and close the deal.

What you are looking for is someone who can do what

you do. Remember, there are only two reasons other than spiritual why a person won't network the kingdom. One is the emotional strain, and the other is that he or she is not teachable.

If a person has been with you to three or four Coffee Shop Meetings, and has read *Networking the Kingdom* and listened to the first six tapes, he's usually either ready or he's kidding you. He either hasn't read the book and listened to the tapes, or he needs a little more time to incubate.

You don't turn everything over to him at once. Begin by transferring more and more leadership to him. Let him get some little successes.

Let the blossoming leader take over the leadership at the potlucks. Soon you stop going with him on some of his recruiting meetings. You begin to challenge him to launch out more and more. Take more and more of his props away from him.

Have you ever watched a mother bird teach her little birds to fly? If they don't fly, she pushes them off the branch.

Timing

> There is a tide in the affairs of men, which,
> taken at the flood, leads on to fortune. . . .
> —William Shakespeare

Sometimes the timing just isn't right for a potential team leader to take on that responsibility. We have to be sensitive to that. Keep in touch with those people. Life is a long time, and situations change.

I remember calling a fellow who worked for a funeral home as a lot salesman. When I asked him to help me part-time with my business, he said, "My boss required me to sign a no-competition contract when I came to work for him."

I couldn't figure out how helping me part-time was going to be in competition with the funeral home, unless his boss thought I would work him to death.

I kept the fellow's name and filed it away for future use. About a year later, he showed up downline in my organization. His situation had changed.

I said, "Nice to have you aboard. What happened?" He said, "I buried a man in the wrong hole. My situation changed." He now has a very large network. The first time, the timing wasn't right. It was this time.

The years teach much which the days never know.
—Ralph Waldo Emerson

One-Winged Angels

In my downline there are two women who are partners. They piddled with their networking business for a while. One day they got turned on and have since built a very large business.

One evening I was sitting in an audience when one of them was speaking to a couple of thousand people. She said, "I had to do something. My situation was desperate. I had two children. My husband ran off with a door-to-door, multi-level hairspray saleswoman."

When they started their group, about all the group had was the ability to love one another and to bond with each other. That's usually enough anywhere, isn't it? They harvested those two talents and received big dividends. I call them my "one-winged angels," because they probably could never have flown if they hadn't locked wings with each other. What do you think?

Look for leaders. Try to make leaders out of all of your team members. Every now and then you'll find someone who is just unteachable. Sometimes you feel like the fellow who said, "Don't ever try to teach a pig to sing. It frustrates you, and it's hard on the pig." Some people are just cantankerous. I teach my people to get away from those types, and let someone else handle them. We can love them, but we don't have to roll around in the mud with them.

But don't forget to keep a record of those you think can someday do it. And don't forget to keep checking back. I don't mean to bug them, but keep in touch. Send them a card from Peter Island, or some other vacation spot. What if I hadn't checked back on the last two associates I told you about?

That is why networking is not a quick fix. In both of the above cases, it was at least a year before either was ready to do something. What if I had quit? That's frightening. Good lesson.

There is a saying that says, "When the pupil is ready, the professor appears." If you are the professor, you don't want to be on your sabbatical the day that special student comes to class.

The Mother Giraffe

A physician and ski buddy of mine from Austin, Texas, told me a story that illustrates what goes on between a team leader and a future team leader.

He said, "When a mother giraffe gives birth, she will poke at the baby giraffe until it gets up. If it doesn't, she gently kicks and pokes at it until it does. If it falls down, she keeps poking at it until it gets up. If it doesn't get on its feet, the predators will get it."

If we don't keep nudging and poking at our new team members, the greatest of predators, the Devil, may get them.

That's why we keep poking at them, gently nudging them to make one more call, read one more verse, say "Hello" to one more person, or write one more card to a future friend for our network. It is our desire that they will begin to transfer this leadership downline. When this happens, we have cloned ourselves.

Don't think that all will respond. The best we can expect is that one in seven will become a leader. We hope all will. We give one hundred percent of our team a chance.

A friend of mine from California who has a large network says, "You can't pull another up over the cliff, until you let go of the hand of the one you just helped up and over the cliff."

We don't like to be weaned. You will have some touchy moments when this happens. Sometimes the new team leader gets jealous that the old team leader is off spending all his time with that new group.

Sometimes the old team leader thinks, "They took my group and now I have to start all over."

While each is partly right, they are mostly wrong, especially in purpose, intent, and attitude.

The old team leader still is an advisor to the new team leader. He just doesn't have the day-to-day responsibility of training, guiding, promoting, and planning that team leader's group. The church and its staff do that now.

The church should take care how this is handled. Remember, when you get seventy-five in a team, a unit, that team should move directly under the guidance and leadership of the church, automatically. Review "When Do the Teams Break Away from Their Team Leader?" in chapter 6.

Marketing companies give leaders who break away a title and a raise or bonus at this point. That sure makes it smooth. The church might give them a title, also, and a banquet. Here are suggested divisions similar to how a marketing company might do it, based on volume. You understand that I am substituting numbers of people for business volume because the Lord counts people and not business volume when He checks His books. Business volume is always used as the criterion in marketing companies.

DIVISIONS BY NUMBERS OF PEOPLE

ONE: A unit is an organization containing seventy-five people divided among three teams with twenty-five on each team.

TWO: Three teams with a unit (seventy-five people) in each team.

THREE: Six teams with a unit in each team.

FOUR: Nine teams with a unit in each team.

FIVE: Twelve teams with a unit in each team.

Twelve teams should do us. I know Someone else who had twelve on His team.

Often, if you make a friend, you make a team leader. You never have a team leader without making a friend.

How Do You Know When to Wean a Team Member?

When I start a new team member, I "move in with him," so to speak, for about ninety days. I am like his shadow. I teach him everything I know, until he is sick of me.

You heard about the pastor who left the church because of his health, didn't you? They were sick and tired of him.

Everyone asks, "How do you know when to wean a team member?" I can tell when someone needs to be weaned. They won't let me talk at the Coffee Shop Meeting. At the first meeting, they just watch and listen and say nothing. Then I ease them into the presentation until they do it all. Now I have cloned myself.

Don't Wean Them Too Soon

Sometimes there is a tendency to wean team members too soon. It's hard to know. It's better to keep them too long than not long enough. Better to err on the side of mothering them too long. It's never "cut and dried" anyway, is it?

Do you remember what happened when the two boys used the tweezers to help the caterpillar out of the cocoon so it could become a butterfly more quickly? They killed it.

Oh! But what a lesson on weaning team members. We need to be careful not to pick our harvest "green." The fruit will fall off the limb when it's ripe.

If your team members stay in the nest too long, though,

they may get to flogging each other. When they do, tell them to go build their own nest: a team of seven new members.

The Verbal Portion of the Brain

> You are searching for the magic key that will unlock the door to the source of power; and yet you have the key in your own hands, and you may make use of it the moment you learn to control your thoughts.
> —Napoleon Hill

If psychologists are right, and I believe they are, the verbal portion of the brain is the strongest. Therefore we ought to be careful of what we say, hear, and think.

Napoleon Hill wrote a best-seller entitled *Think and Grow Rich*. He must have read Proverbs 23:7, which says, "As he thinketh in his heart, so is he." I teach my associates to be around the kind of people they want to be like. I like people who think and say good thoughts. I like positive people.

I had just returned with one of my University groups, the Heritage Singers, from a U.S.O. tour to Greenland, Iceland, Newfoundland, and Labrador. We were asked to do a show where Paul Harvey was to be the guest speaker. It was my assignment and pleasure to pick him up at his hotel. When I knocked on his door, he opened the door, and said, with a great big smile, "Good morning, America!"

I don't like to be around negative people. It doesn't mean they are bad; I just don't like to listen to them. If you are going to do what your subconscious mind tells you to do, tell it to do good things.

Someone said, it's as if Jesus were saying to us, "My people say what they have, but I tell them they can have what they say." That's the poetic version. These are His exact words:

> You do not get what you want because you do not ask God.
> —James 4:2

Watch Out for Job's Friends

Job was in a mess. Everything that could go wrong had. Do you remember when his friends came by, and said:

> You should just curse God and die!
> —Job 2:9

Do you have any friends like that? Now, that's no way to talk to a friend when he's down and out. Actually, I think it was his wife. Anyway old Job looked up through tear filled eyes and said:

> I know that my redeemer liveth,
> and that he shall stand at the latter day upon the earth:
>   And though . . . worms destroy this body,
> yet in my flesh shall I see God.
> —Job 19:25–26 (King James Version)

Which words came true? The ones Job said. Remember, you can be "hung by the tongue." If you don't want it to come true, don't say it. If you don't want it in your subconscious, don't listen.

I know a woman who is at the pinnacle of success in networking. She and her husband are called Crown Ambassadors. It isn't important that you know what that means, but it is real good. When something negative comes up, she excuses herself and moves. If someone with her vast empire feels that strongly, how can we, who are lesser lights, take the chance?

You're a team leader. Here comes one of Job's friends right up to you, and says, "All you're doing is getting a bunch of new people into the church. They aren't doing anything. Not one of them sings in the choir, teaches Sunday School, or tithes."

"What do you say to him?" I know what you want to say, but we can't do that.

I remember a story of two men who went bear hunting.

One got scared and told his friend, "I think I'll stay here in the cabin and cook supper while you go look for a bear."

The other one didn't like the deal, but didn't want to let his friend know he was scared, too. So he took his gun, and just as he rounded the first bend, met up with a great big bear standing on his hind legs, staring right at him.

He dropped his gun and hightailed it for the cabin, the bear gaining on him all the way. Just as he reached the cabin, he misjudged the first step and fell. The bear's momentum took him right over the top of him and through the front door.

The man jumped up, pulled the door shut, and yelled to his friend, "There he is. Kill him and cook him. I'm going back after another one."

You feel like saying to Job's friends, "Kill him and cook him. I'm going back after another one."

You never really know exactly what to say, because it is sort of a putdown. What I say is, "How much were they tithing, singing in the choir, and teaching before they came into the church?" They couldn't. They didn't even know about our church.

We of Team Seven did that part of the job. Now it's up to all of us to disciple them.

Watch out for Job's friends. They may be well-poisoners. They'll "Yeah, but . . ." you and "If only . . ." you to death. When they come to you, "What if?"

Sometimes how we hear things makes a difference in how we respond. Back in Tennessee, I heard about a preacher who was having dinner with one of the deacons at a church where he was in "view of a call."

The deacon asked him if he'd like some more corn, and the preacher passed his glass.

It's only words. But sometimes words conjure up different meanings to different people, don't they?

I have compared the transferring of leadership from one team leader to a new team leader to the weaning process between a mother and her offspring. Sometimes a team leader

gets to thinking that the new team members are his or hers.
Not so. They belong to Another. Kahlil Gibran makes a
profound point on the subject:

> Your children are not your children.
> They are the sons and daughters of Life's longing for
>   itself.
> They come through you but not from you,
> And though they are with you they belong not to you.
> You may give them your love but not your thoughts,
> For they have their own thoughts.
> You may house their bodies but not their souls,
> For their souls dwell in the house of tomorrow, which
>   you cannot visit, not even in your dreams.
> You may strive to be like them, but seek not to make
>   them like you.
> For life goes not backward nor tarries with yesterday.
> You are the bow from which your children as living
>   arrows are sent forth.
> The archer sees the mark upon the path of the infinite,
>   and He bends you with His might that His arrow
>   may go swift and far.
> Let your bending in the archer's hand be for gladness;
> For even as He loves the arrow that flies, so He loves
>   also the bow that is stable.[1]

13

Babies Cry for It and Men Die for It

We are all motivated by a keen desire for praise, and the better a man is, the more he is inspired by glory. The very philosophers themselves, even in those books which they write in contempt of glory, inscribe their names.
—Marcus Tullius Cicero

Scott and I were talking about the Team Seven concept with a friend who teaches evangelism at a seminary. He said, "How are you going to motivate the people to do this?"

Good question.

Because this area is as personal as your toothbrush, I have to be careful. So rather than telling you what to do, I think I'll process our thinking through a series of things we already know to do when we are trying to get someone to do something.

In my business, money alone is not the primary motivator. I have people who have all the money they will ever need. Why would they work, then? One big reason is that they like the recognition that comes from achieving a certain level in the business.

I've seen physicians literally weep as they walked off the stage for having been recognized for reaching the fifteen-percent level in our business. That was something they earned. At the hospital, a person doesn't jump up and down because the doctor took his appendix out. Same for lawyers and other professionals.

I heard a Canadian networker say of recognition: "Babies cry for it and men die for it."

Give Special Recognition to Your Team Leaders

I have fought the good fight. I have finished the race. I have kept the faith.

Now, a crown is waiting for me. I will get that crown for being right with God. The Lord is the judge who judges rightly, and he will give me the crown on that day.

—2 Timothy 4:7–8

It is my recommendation that as soon as one becomes a team leader, meaning that he has built a team of seven new church members, he should be honored, publicly. How? You figure it out. As I said earlier, perhaps have all seven of his new families sit together on Sunday morning and stand to be recognized. Or have a team leader banquet.

After they get a team, seven deep, we give our team leaders a choice between one of our "Team Seven T-Shirts" or a "Team Seven Lapel Pin."

That might not seem like much of a big deal to you. But tomorrow when you go to work, notice how many people are wearing a lapel pin of some sort or another. It means something to them.

How long has it been since you saw a T-shirt without a message on it? I can't remember the last time I saw one. In Tennessee, we have a saying, "It's not a barn unless it has a 'See Rock City' sign on it." People love message T-shirts.

If you don't like those suggestions, use your own creativity (not on the pins and shirts for the trademarks are copy-righted). But give them something tangible that they can feel and touch. It's the thought. It's also because they can touch it and show it off. Give them recognition in proportion to what they earned.

When someone sends me a postcard from some exotic place in the world encouraging me, I put it up at our business center for all of my associates to see. After about two months, when I think everyone has seen it, I take it home and put it on my refrigerator. After I get ketchup on it, I put it in my box of treasures. You say, "But that's crazy!" Yeah. I know it. But I have a lot of friends who do, too. Try it.

We as church leaders have been long on asking for help and making great demands of our members, but we have been short on saying, "Thanks for a job well done." Remember: What gets rewarded gets done.

Who among us has not said, on Mother's Day, "Will the oldest mother please stand? Now will the youngest mother please stand?"

Who among us hasn't said on New Year's Sunday, "All you new parents, bring your new baby down to the front for a prayer"?

Who among us has not said on Friends' Day, "Will all of you who brought a friend please stand to be recognized?"

"Will all the new deacons and their wives please stand to be recognized?"

"Today we are going to recognize our education director and his family. It is his fifth anniversary."

What happens if you forget your spouse's anniversary?

Why do we like to get birthday cards?

Who would refuse a request to sit at the captain's table on a cruise?

What would the pastor think, if on his first anniversary, he and his family were not recognized? "Time to look for another church" is what he'd probably think, and he'd probably be right. "What a bunch of ingrates."

Detractors

Allow them to eat at your table.
They helped me. . . .
                    —1 Kings 2:7

You're down in the fellowship hall of the church setting up
tables for the Team Seven Banquet. You have three new
members who have their teams seven deep, and they are
going to be recognized as new team leaders at 8:00 tonight.
It's 5:30 and the janitor didn't get it done. The ladies are
there to decorate, but they need help with the tables. You're
thinking, "When they called me to be pastor, I didn't know
I'd have to be janitor, too."

About that time the phone rings. It's your wife. She's
downtown and the car has a flat. She called a service station,
but the dog jumped out of the car, and she can't find it. You
call a deacon to come and help with the tables, so you can go
help your wife find the dog.

Before you can get out the door, another call for you. Your
secretary says in a knowing voice, "It's him."

You're standing there with your dust rag in your hand,
your shirt tail half out, and white perspiration stains coming
through the armpits of your best blue suit, and your wife is
downtown with a flat and a lost dog, and this is the second
time today he's called. He's been on your back about one
thing or another ever since you came here. It's the "well-
poisoner." Every church has one. Some have two.

On such occasions, the Devil gets in us and we feel like
responding in kind. But we don't. Patiently you sizzle as he
dresses you down.

He says, "You're putting too much emphasis on numbers. You're putting too much emphasis on recognition. I
do everything I do for the Lord; I don't want any recognition. I don't think you should either. You shouldn't be
spending the church's money on banquets to brag on people. You ought to be bragging on the Lord." They always
use part truths, don't they? As you look down the list of

those to be recognized tonight, you notice his name is not on there. What do you say? I don't know. But let's look at the problem.

I think sometimes, in our effort at being humble, we forget that we are also human. I can't help it; I just like a good old pat on the back. I know others do, too. How about you?

Let me tell you why I spoke out so strongly. I've had any number of people, who were not scheduled to be recognized because they hadn't done anything, say, "I think you are placing too much emphasis on recognition by letting them walk across the stage and tell their stories."

I have never seen anyone who had earned the recognition who wasn't waiting with bated breath for his name to be called for his time in the sun. No exceptions. *No exceptions.* That's why I know people are usually kidding me, or themselves, when they say, "I don't like being recognized."

Not always, but sometimes what they are really saying is either, "I haven't done anything to be recognized for," or "I don't plan to do anything to be recognized for." And sometimes they are so "eat up with humbleitis" that they really believe the Lord wouldn't want anyone to be given recognition in the church. They have the right to their opinion, but let us have ours, also.

Evidently, Paul didn't see anything wrong with honoring those who had faithfully labored. Listen to what happened on one of his missionary journeys:

> The people on the island gave us many honors. . . . When we were ready to leave, they gave us the things we needed.
> —Acts 28:10

In sales school, at the Southwestern Company, they taught us, "People have two reasons for anything: one reason that sounds good and the real reason."

When people jump on me about recognition like that fellow did the pastor a while ago, I say to them, "Go ahead and do it for the Lord then, and that will be okay." But then they never refuse the recognition.

Whose name do you like to hear best? Whose name do you look for first when you know yours is printed there somewhere? Whose picture do you look for first when the ski photos or Christmas photos come back? You see, there is nothing wrong with that. And God knows we are like that. Edgar Watson Howe said:

> The greatest humiliation in life is to work hard on something from which you expect great appreciation, and then fail to get it.

It Still Depends on How Hungry the Donkey Is

Even though we may dangle all sorts of carrots in the form of recognition and attention in front of our team members, it is still up to them as to what they will or won't do. God speaks of some pretty significant prizes He offers, too: salvation, eternal life, a home in Heaven, and a crown with stars in it. My point is not whether or not our work earns them, but that He has rewards awaiting us.

It doesn't matter how many carrots are dangled in front of the donkey; it still depends on how hungry the donkey is. And our biggest challenge always has been and always will be, how to get the donkey hungry enough to pull the load he is supposed to pull.

G. K. Chesterton tells the story of the triumphal entry of Jesus into the city of Jerusalem on Palm Sunday. But he writes it from the donkey's viewpoint.

Sometimes we also get mixed up and think the palm branches are for us. Sometimes we complain that we'd rather ride than bear the load assigned to us.

As we recognize a team leader for a job well done, let's be careful not to get mixed up and place more emphasis on the worker than we do on the Master. But in our carefulness, let's remember to give the donkey the carrot we dangled in front of him.

Psychologists tell us that it is important to keep our

promises to ourselves. If we promise ourselves a reward for reaching a certain goal, it is important to give the reward when the goal is reached. If we don't, our psyche stops believing us. The next time we call on our subconscious mind to reach a goal, it says to us, "Whom do you think you are kidding?" You see, it is even important that we give recognition to ourselves.

If this is so, how much more important is it that we recognize those we've asked to help us network the kingdom, when they do a good job?

C.S. Lewis makes an important point about self-denial and rewards:

> The New Testament has lots to say about self-denial, but not about self-denial as an end in itself. We are told to deny ourselves and to take up our crosses in order that we may follow Christ; and nearly every description of what we shall ultimately find if we do so contains an appeal to desire. If there lurks in most modern minds the notion that to desire our own good and earnestly to hope for the enjoyment of it is a bad thing, I submit that this notion has crept in from Kant and the Stoics and is no part of the Christian faith. Indeed if we consider the unblushing promises of reward and the staggering nature of the rewards promised in the Gospels, it would seem that Our Lord finds our desires, not too strong, but too weak. We are half-hearted creatures, fooling about with drink and sex and ambition when infinite joy is offered us, like an ignorant child who wants to go on making mud pies in a slum because he cannot imagine what is meant by the offer of a holiday at the sea. We are far too easily pleased.[1]

Who Begat Whom?

> Adam begat. . . .
> —Genesis 5:3 (King James Version)

It is important that the church keep records on the lines of sponsorship. We need to know who begat whom. If you don't have a better system, you can just use the one God used in Genesis 5:3. He tells how "Adam begat. . . ."

Whatever record keeping system you are using, just plug your Team Seven genealogy into that. In the business world, a person is given a computer number when he joins us. It also has his sponsor's name and computer number on the enrollment form. That way the computer can track the lineage throughout the world.

The simplest solution would be to have each new team member fill out an extra card at the time he and his family join the church. It could be very simple. Just show his sponsor's number and assign him a number when he joins. Mail him a card, or let him call the church to get the assigned Team Seven number. Do not fill in the line of sponsorship for the new team member on the spot. Let the secretary do that from the computer. When the new team member joins the church, he may not be directly under his friend. Two or three names may have already been added.

I think that it is important that you use some kind of tracking method of genealogy, or else it turns into the same old everybody's business is nobody's business.

When I was a youngster, I had a cousin back in Cleveland, Tennessee, who used to play his guitar and sing a then popular, Stamps-Baxter gospel song on the Evening Light Tabernacle Radio Show. His name was Penny, and the song's title was, "My Lord Keeps a Record."

If the church doesn't "keep a record," we know Who will. We know where He keeps it too, don't we? It's in the *Lamb's Book of Life.*

14

A Word to the Pastor

There are those who travel and those who are going somewhere. They are different and yet they are the same. The
success has this over his rivals: he knows where he is going.

—Mark Caine

I've seen lazy people. I've met lazy plumbers, pilots, students, networkers, insurance salesmen, and so forth. But I
have never met a lazy preacher. I have never heard of one.
Oh, I've met broken ministers, discouraged and disheart-
ened, but even those; if they had a plan in place, would burn
themselves out day or night. Some have been to all the
church growth conferences and all the seminars, and their
churches still aren't growing. They are probably beginning
to ask themselves the big question, "How do you get the
right combination?"

The Right Occupation But the
Wrong Combination

I imagine, if the truth were known, there are a lot of pastors
and other church leaders out there who feel that they have

the right occupation but the wrong combination. I had a good pastor friend say to me one time, "Most ministers resign every Monday morning."

I know you, Joe Pastor; I know your heart. I know you who have great big churches and you who have little bitty churches. The thing I know best about you is that you'd be doing something else if you did not believe to your dying breath that God is in what you are doing, or trying to do.

I know you have as many bosses as you have members, and you are on the firing line every day. I know how you feel when you've been up all night with a teenager because he's afraid to go home. You take him home, and the father stands there and cusses you out.

I know that many times you feel like the fellow who was going door to door witnessing. One elegant lady, as he witnessed to her, gave him a piece of her mind for knocking on her door.

He stood on her porch and wept and sang:

> But drops of grief can ne'er repay
> The debt of love I owe:
> Here, Lord, I give myself away,
> 'Tis all that I can do![1]

God's Briar Patch

I have two very important questions to ask you right now, and I don't mean either one disrespectfully. I don't know how to bring up the subject without just coming right out and asking you. "If God had something new and fresh to say to you, how hard would it be for Him to get your attention?"

My second question. "What other plan in the history of the church has ever even claimed to offer you a chance to double last year's net growth in one year?" Who would have considered the possibility of doubling the entire membership in one year? Staggering, isn't it?

I know you thought that God would send the suggestions

by way of some theological giant, some expert in church growth, or some leading pastor, but all you got was me. I didn't have time either, but somehow He got through all the hustle and bustle of my life. He sure took me through some briar patches before He told me where He was taking me, though.

When you're out there in God's briar patch, and the chiggers are biting, the briars are pricking you, and the copperheads are hissing, it's kinda hard to see God in that, isn't it? Wonder why He does things like that?

I can think of two good reasons we are sometimes put in God's briar patch. Have you ever tried to get out of a briar patch?

1. You don't get in a hurry, and
2. You don't sit down.

I would have thought He would have chosen some hall of higher learning to disperse His message about networking the kingdom. But He didn't. It's sort of funny, isn't it? Who would have thought of Him speaking from a briar patch? Wasn't it Moses He talked to from a burning bush? I guess it's not so funny after all, is it?

He told Moses, "Take your shoes off. . . ." But I don't think He said that to me 'cause I wasn't wearing any.

Doesn't it seem strange that the King of Heaven would choose to use us as the vehicles of His message and grace, after the knotholes He has pulled us through?

His way may "twist and turn," but He has a plan. This verse helps, doesn't it?

> I have good plans for you. . . .
> I will bring you back from your captivity.
> —Jeremiah 29:11–14

I know a little of how He must have felt, trying to get my attention. I had the same difficulty with a pastor friend. He is very important, but I called him up anyway to ask him if he would have a cup of coffee with me so I could get his counsel on how to use Team Seven in the church.

From the very beginning, I had some idea of the magnitude of what Team Seven could do in the reclamation of the kingdom. I remembered someone saying, "There is much wisdom in many counselors." I didn't want to blow it. So I did due diligence.

Did you know, it wasn't easy to get you fellows' attention? I'm not talking about now. I'm talking about then. Someday when I know you better I will tell you more. Of those from whom I sought counsel, I must tell you that 99.99 percent of them were waiting with bated breath.

Anyway, the pastor returned my call from the airport. I could hear them announcing the departures and arrivals of the flights. I explained what I needed, and he said, "Brother, I'm at the airport flying to Atlanta for a very important meeting. I'm up to my hips in alligators at my church, trying to raise the budget for this next year, and I don't have time to look at anything or talk to anyone. Call me in three or four months after I get through this budget campaign." Click.

A long time ago we had had coffee together. He had no reason to set an appointment to talk to me. I understand that. And he would have talked to me under other circumstances. He is a good man and the best of preachers.

It was that conversation, though, that made me ask the question, "If God had something new and fresh to say to you, how hard would it be for Him to get your attention?"

I Don't Want a Quarter-Inch Drill; I Want a Quarter-Inch Hole

Has it been your experience that it is as hard to find prospects for your church as it is to find the next page in the *Reader's Digest?* If so, as the Team Seven concept is unfolded before you, you may feel like yelling "Eureka," or something.

Your problem with Team Seven will be that you may recruit new members so fast that you "outrun your headlights."

You need to recruit and then take a period of time to bond and teach. Then hit it again.

How many are too many? How many can you harvest and not upset the applecart? I'm not being funny, because if you double your membership in a year using Team Seven (and if you work at it at all, you may be able to do that), half of your membership will only know what you taught them that year.

We know of instances where large numbers came, like after one of Peter's sermons:

> About 3,000 people were added to the number of believers that day.
> —Acts 2:41

But we are talking here about harvesting day in and day out 365 days a year, where the fruit is picked daily and brought into the storehouse one at a time. Of course there are a lot of "ones" getting a lot of other "ones."

Your biggest problem will come from people abusing your teachings of how to apply the concept. "Some people are like blotters: They soak up everything but get it backwards."

Did you hear the one about the knight who went east instead of west? He came running in to give his report to the king and said, "We've been pillaging and killing your enemies in the east."

The king said, "My enemies are in the west. I don't have any enemies in the east."

"You do now."

So you, as the pastor, must not farm this out to a "hireling." If you are not there in the trenches, it may get away from you, because it goes so fast. Remember what happened to the Valdez when the captain wasn't on the bridge. Disaster. The worst oil spill in history.

Beware of so-called "networking experts." Many are multi-level junkies who flit from starting one new company to the next. This is probably the worst type you can get to be a team leader. I, of course, am not talking about those with legitimate companies. You can find out real fast with two questions. One, "How long have you been with your net-working company?" and two, "How long has that company been in business?" Enough said.

Another problem will come from people who are fantastic at recruiting, but they bring the people to the church and dump them. There is a type of intoxication that some people get from the excitement of the explosion. You must insist that they bond and teach. You will have to force them to go more slowly. Who would have thought it? Tell our members, "Don't bring so many so fast." Wow.

Team Seven may not be what you were looking for. If you are like most church leaders, you were desiring growth through traditional means. Did you know that Sears sold thousands of quarter-inch drills last year to customers who didn't want a quarter-inch drill? They wanted a quarter-inch hole.

You don't have to have a desire to implement Team Seven. It is enough that you want church growth. Team Seven may give you the growth you desire.

You may have to struggle with the concept for a while, but you may want to try "A New Way of Struggling," as defined by Susan W. N. Ruach:

> To struggle used to be
> To grab with both hands
>   and shake
>   and twist
>   and turn
>   and push
>   and shove and not give in
> But wrest an answer from it all
> As Jacob did a blessing.
>   But there is another way
> To struggle with an issue, a question—
> Simply to jump
>   off
>   into the abyss
>   and find ourselves
>   floating

> falling
> tumbling
> being led
> slowly and gently
> but surely
> to the answers God has for us—
> to watch the answers unfold
> before our eyes and still
> to be a part of the unfolding.
> But, oh! the trust
> necessary for this new way!
> Not to be always reaching out
> For the old hand-holds.[2]

I don't know how long you are to struggle before you let go and say, "Let's go for it." But I know one thing. If you see this, you won't sleep tonight. And if you don't see it, it won't matter, anyway.

I cannot take you where I have not been, and I cannot take you if you will not go. But at this point, the Team Seven concept is so new, you stand as good a chance as anyone of becoming a superstar on earth and in Heaven. No matter what your situation, even if you are a student just out of seminary with no church, you may be only months away from an empire.

Pick out a good spot with lots of hurting people and build your own church. Start in a home. Find three people and make each of them into a unit, and you have 225 people. Because of the geometric progression of networking, you can pack fifty years of traditional growth into five years.

Start now, though. Tomorrow will steal it from you. Do everything exactly as I have taught you, and you'll do all right. Go claim your mountain! One pastor said:

Oh, to be a recent seminary graduate with a copy of *Networking the Kingdom* under my arm, a bag full of the six starter tapes, a car that would run, God on my side, and the world to choose from for my pastorate.

I was visiting with another pastor about Team Seven, and he said, "Wow! We were already planning to add a new staff member and put him in charge of 'church growth.' I want to hear more about Team Seven."

I didn't have the heart to tell him, but his remark reminded me of the conversation I overheard some seminary professors having one day. One professor said, "Yes. We were going to offer a course in 'Common Sense,' but we couldn't find anyone to teach it."

I wondered who was going to teach the fellow a class in church growth. Church growth is more than a class, isn't it? That's like saying, "We're going to have a class at the seminary on 'How to Be a Preacher.'" The subject is too broad for one class, and church growth seems to be what the entire staff and membership do, not just one staff member.

I know that some churches get together and have church growth conferences, but the conferences usually involve a myriad of talents and events. I know that some church growth conferences evolve around some personality, rather than any new principles of growth, but that's the exception. Most of those conferences are like diets. If they worked, there wouldn't be but one. What do you think?

Not a Model Airplane Set: More Like a Lego Set

If it is any consolation to you, you probably see in Team Seven something completely different from the pastor whose church field joins yours.

Team Seven is like a mirror; everyone sees something different in it.

Some leaders try to make the concept rigid and formal. They want everyone to do it exactly the same. They want the team to come out looking like a model airplane set. If all teams of seven don't look exactly alike, they say, "You have put the model airplane together wrong."

I tell people, "It's not like a model airplane set. It's more like a Lego set. You make out of it what you want to."

The Difference Between
Knowledge and Skill

Concerning networking, here is the most serious error I have seen pastors and other leaders make. There is a false sense of confidence that comes with a little bit of information about networking. It looks so simple and easy. It is that false sense of confidence that causes people to go out and start their own networking companies and fall flat on their faces. Then they say, "Networking doesn't work."

Here is the problem. Because a person understands networking intellectually, after having had it explained to him, he often misjudges the skills required to network. It looks so simple. It is simple, but it is not easy. The skills require a lifetime to master.

Even serious students may be lulled into thinking that just because they read this book, they are skilled at networking. They may be confused about the differences between understanding networking and having the skills to network. A person gets the understanding from verbal explanations, reading, and listening to tapes, but the skills are developed in the field.

Let me illustrate this for you. Recently, I was at a potluck dinner for our Sunday School department. I had just been introduced as a former music professor to a lady who was a visitor. She had a wonderful personality and a quick wit. In fact, I was having difficulty staying with her quick responses.

After a while, she said, "Do you know how to play the piano?"

I said, "Yes," knowing what the response would be. I had been through this before.

She pointed to the piano, and said, "Why don't you play something for us?"

To which I replied, "I can't play the piano."

She said, "You just said you know how to play the piano."

I said, "What I meant was I understand how the piano is played, but I do not have the skill to play it. There is a difference between knowing how the piano is played and having the skill to do so."

Many people will be that way about *Networking the Kingdom*. They will read the book and say, "I know all about networking." They will know a lot. But knowing about networking and having the skills to network are as different as knowing how a piano is played and having the skill to play the piano.

Take the time to develop the skills. Don't judge yourself too harshly too soon. Give yourself time to grow and to let your people grow.

When I taught composition at the university, the biggest problem my students had was that they judged their fragile efforts at creativity by the standards of the compositions that had been written by the master composers.

There is no telling how many magnificent unfinished symphonies have been thrown into the trash can because the student misjudged his work too soon or had a friend who did. (There were also a few that should have been thrown into the trash can but weren't.)

The Enemy to the Great Church Is the Good Church

I teach my business associates a statement by a physician friend of mine from California who is also very successful in network marketing. He says, "The enemy of the great life is the good life." A lot of people have enough income to get by, and they will never venture out in order to have a great lifestyle.

Some churches are satisfied with the number of members they have. Some entire denominations have made that decision, too. That's okay. They're just not the ones we are addressing here. We're looking for pastors who want their churches to grow.

There are a lot of good churches around, but it is my opinion that the enemy of the great church is the good church. Being large does not mean being great.

More Outlets

"What if? What if the church could adopt one principle that McDonald's uses?" McDonald's knows that their growth is dependent upon opening more outlets. The reason they sell more hamburgers than other hamburger chains is because they have more outlets. Other chains sell about as many as McDonald's does per outlet.

How does the church open more outlets? Every team leader is an outlet. Get more team leaders.

"What if? What if we quit thinking of the limits of the walls of the building and how far our church field is supposed to extend?"

"What if? What if it didn't matter where a team leader was located?" You say, "Oh, but that's out of my church field. I can't harvest over there." Who said so? "What if?" Oh well, you finish that thought. But turn loose and dream.

You know what the most frustrating thing is about reading a good uplifting positive book on how to get involved in some business or venture? Down in the little bitty footnote on the last page in small print, this great big fantastic comment: "First, you need a vehicle."

Team Seven may be your vehicle. Just because you don't know how to drive it yet doesn't mean you can't get it out and back it up and down the driveway. Watch out, though. As soon as you give it a "kick start" by helping a member find his first "Andrew," it goes flying off on its own. Zoom. . . .

When you get a strong driver for the vehicle, you lead him just like you do an elephant. Do you know how to lead a wild elephant? You grab hold of his hind leg and hold on.

Could you handle a whole herd of Team Seven elephants? They don't cost you a dime, and you don't have to feed them. You've got to catch the first one; then he catches and calms the herd. "What if?" You take it from there.

Many times we are bound up by: "What might have been," "Almost," "We never did it that way," "Who do you think you are to be recommending such an idea to us?" and "Let's play the Devil's advocate for a minute." Too often we stifle our own potential for greatness.

Some of your people will bombard you with, "Yeah, but this" and, "Yeah, but that." Others will say, "If only this," and, "If only that." I quote them an old Chinese proverb:

> Man who says, "It cannot be done,"
> Should not interrupt man who is doing it.

Your challenge will be to get them to change their thinking from "Yeah, but" and "If only" to "What if?"

The Same Wind Takes One Ship
East and the Other Ship West

> If a man knows not what harbor he seeks,
> any wind is the right wind.
>
> —Seneca

Sometimes I wonder about things. Why is it that two coaches who went to the same school, studied the same plays, and had the same teachers, don't have the same record at the end of their coaching careers? Could we agree that it is not the fault of their training?

Why is it that two pastors who went to the same seminary, had the same professors, read the same book and heard the same tapes on Team Seven, and whose church fields join, don't have the same growth? Could we agree that it has little to do with location?

Why is it that one ship reaches harbor two hours before the other, both having left the same port at the same time and using the same wind? The wise captain has his eye on the goal and seizes every opportunity to make the proper tack. The foolish captain keeps looking back to see if his dinghy is still secured, in case he has to head for shore.

Why is it that the same wind takes one ship east and the other ship west?

One ship sails east and another west
While the self-same breezes blow:
"Tis the set of the sail and not the gale
That bids them where to go."
—Unknown

I Can Find Seven Who Want to Live

I don't know if Team Seven will work in your situation or not. But what is more important, you don't either. What if it did work? What would ten teams of seven do to infuse new life into your church? You understand that that is ten teams of seven families; with an average of three to a family that's 210 people.

I don't know about you. But if that Rev. Jim Jones could talk over two hundred people into killing themselves, I know I can find seven people who want to live. How about you?

How many pulpit committees would be at your church next month if your church were doubling every year? How many conventions or revivals would you be asked to speak for? What if you had to get another pair of wading boots, because you wore the other pair out baptizing people? What a thought. Okay. I know some of you sprinkle.

What if your church grew to seven times its current size in a year or seven years? What would your church budget be? What if you could make spiritual decisions for other than financial reasons? What if?

Of course I don't know that it will do that. If your church is growing as fast as you want it to, you may not need Team Seven. There's an old saying, "If it ain't broke, don't fix it." I am not talking to "those who are whole," but to "those who are sick," who "need a physician."

I do know that if we don't implement Team Seven, we force our churches to stay on their present growth curve. Our only alternative is to continue to do what we've always done.

Your church may be growing fast enough. That's fantastic. You may be growing so fast that you would respond like one associate pastor did who said to me, "Where do you think we'd put the people? All we need is to double in size. We have to have our members park blocks away now and ride a bus to church."

I know that there are churches that are growing like that. I've been in them. But I am not sure that that is the right attitude. I think, "To whom much is given, much is expected." What do you think?

I know that there are churches that are favorably located geographically, or that have pastors with leadership skills and charisma, that are having exceptional growth. I also know that these are usually exceptions to the rule. If that's your case, may your tribe increase. You may be doubling in size every year already, and you feel Team Seven would slow you down.

I know some pastors of great and extremely large churches whose hearts burn with a desire to double and even triple in size. They want to reach even more people. Imagine that. All you have to do is to listen to the fire in their voices when they get on the subject. I've seen this fire in their eyes as they talk of growing and reaching more and more people.

When you leave them, you feel like the two disciples on the way to Emmaus must have felt after Jesus had just left them. They hadn't recognized Him at first. They said:

When Jesus talked to us on the road, it felt like a fire burning in us.

—Luke 24:32

I bet some of the wives are saying, "Lord, don't you think enough's enough? If you do give us a bigger harvest, don't make him harvest on our family day that we have just for us. And Lord, if you send an increased harvest, please send more reapers. My man's doing about all he can do."

If I know "Joe Pastor's" heart, and I think I do, most pastors would fit into this latter category, whether they have a big church or a little bitty one.

Does it irritate you a little when some staff member who basks in the growth of a dynamic church struts like *he* did it, while the pastor and other staff members are out there breaking their backs for the kingdom? Have you ever noticed that some staff members can strut while they are sitting down? Wonder how they do that?

But Team Seven works regardless of personality or location. If you are in a situation that is stagnant, or you started feeling two years ago that your work was done in that community, and someone forgot to tell God, you are the one I want to talk to.

If you are the kind of person who is wanting to lead people to the Cross, and you've got some members who are trying to nail you to it, you are the one I came to talk to. Team Seven will show you how to pump new blood, not yours, into a congregation. You may be the kind of pastor who says, "All I ever wanted was a chance." Well, this may be your chance. I don't know. Just a thought. You may have lost so many battles that you would just as soon not talk about it. The fact that you are still in the ring says something good about you.

> The man who wins may have been counted out several times, but he didn't hear the referee.
>
> —H. E. Jansen

I have a friend who has a large network as well as a camp for children where they teach the children "positive living" themes. I heard him say one time, "It's not too late for you to become all you ever wanted to be." What a thought. I bet you and he would agree with this statement, "It's not too late for a church to become everything you and God ever wanted it to be." What do you think?

I'll tell you something else, too. If you are ever going to grow a forest, you've got to plant enough trees, or you'll never grow a forest in your lifetime.

Team Seven lets us plant enough trees so we can grow a forest in our lifetime, and then allows us time to sit in the shade of some of the trees.

"Oh, but God might not want us to grow that fast," the well-poisoner says. Let Him tell you that, then. Come to the party. We're not going this way but once.

Who Do You Think Sent Me?

One day I was in a coffee shop talking to a prospect about my business. He was the religious type. After I finished displaying my wares and the opportunity for him to help me part-time, I asked, "If you were going to help me, would you have any problem with any of the things we have discussed here?"

His response: "You already know I lost my bank, my wife left me, and they repossessed my Mercedes. I've been praying that God would send me an opportunity so I could get back on my feet. I'll have to think about this, though. I'm sort of waiting for Him to show me the right thing."

Before I thought, I said, "Who do you think sent me?"

Sometimes we get so engrossed in our everyday ministry that it seems to become commonplace. Humdrum activities cause us to become too hardened to ask, "What if?" God is going to use someone. He's going to do it somewhere. It might as well be you. Here is a plan that lets you use the greatest asset of your church: your people. No money involved, no budget banquet required, no posters, just you, God, and His. He is going about reclaiming His. Let's join His reclamation team.

I know you are working hours past what is required. I hope the Team Seven concept helps you work smart, not hard.

The Fear of Loss Is Greater
Than the Prospect of Gain

The credit belongs to the man who is actually in the arena, whose face is marred by dust and sweat and blood; who strives valiantly; who errs and comes short again and again, who knows the great enthusiasms, the great devotions, and spends himself in a worthy cause; who at the best, knows the triumph of high achievement; and who, at the worst, if he fails, at least fails while daring greatly, so that his place shall never be with those cold and timid souls who know neither victory nor defeat.

—Theodore Roosevelt

Psychologists tell us the fear of loss is greater than the prospect of gain. Some of us are more afraid of what folks would think if we failed, than what our church and the kingdom would gain if it worked. Og Mandino said:

Only a worm is free from the worry of falling.[3]

I have some appreciation for the exposure you have. I know what it means to you if you try a new something or another in your church and it doesn't work. I also know how cruel some of the "brethren" can be. Misery loves company. But "What if? What if it worked?" If it worked, they'd be just as hard on you. "Much praise createth much enmity."

Progress always involves risk; you can't steal second base and keep your foot on first.

—Frederick Wilcox

I've known many great and wonderful pastors who have climbed the heights. I know another group of pastors who labor in love, day in and day out, year in and year out, in the small communities of the world, who have never basked in the sunlight of attention. Nor have they sought to. Good men, great men, but men who never had the chance at the "big-time circuit."

I heard an important composer say one time, "The worst curse God can put on a composer is to make him almost great." The pastors about whom I speak are great; some just haven't enjoyed the attention the world gives its pastors who are the "stars."

Some of these go about their tasks daily, being found faithful. I know these men. I have labored with them and I am their champion. I honor them for we climbed part of the way up the mountain together. I know their names. Some of them. I know a few who even lost their way. And some who lost their families. God knows all their names. I bet you could name a few yourself.

I know another group. There are pastors who will die with their dreams and networks still inside their bosoms because they never found the formula for expressing all the gifts God has given them. Here's hoping Team Seven is their formula. Sir Walter Scott said:

> One hour of life, crowded to the full with glorious action, and filled with noble risks, is worth whole years of those mean observances of paltry decorum in which men steal through existence, like sluggish waters through a marsh, without either honor or observation.

For what it's worth to you, I saw this little bit of information on the refrigerator in the home of a friend of mine. It is titled "The Risk Takers," and it seems to put a lot of things into perspective:

> To laugh is to risk appearing a fool.
> To weep is to risk appearing sentimental.
> To reach out for another is to risk involvement.
> To expose feelings is to risk rejection.
> To place your dreams before the crowd is to risk
>   ridicule.
> To love is to risk not being loved in return.
> To go forward in the face of overwhelming odds is to
>   risk failure.
> But risks must be taken because the greatest
> hazard in life is to risk nothing. The person
> who risks nothing does nothing, has nothing, is
> nothing. He may avoid suffering and sorrow,
> but he cannot learn, feel, change, grow or love.
> Chained by his certitudes, he is a slave. He has
> forfeited his freedom. Only a person who takes
> risks is free.

May I mention another type of risk? I swell with pride when I see our men and women in uniform for our country. I know you do, too. I told you earlier that I toured for the U.S.O. to Greenland, Iceland, Newfoundland, and Labrador. I've sat with those men at the monitor screens in Tule, Greenland, where our early warning missile system is located with a red phone that is a direct line to the President of the United States of America. Those brave men are on guard there tonight as we talk.

If you don't want to try the Team Seven concept, it's okay. You may already have your boat loaded. I also understand that this may not be your cup of tea. That's okay, too. Let's be friends, anyway.

If you do decide to dream, pick out a big one. "Small dreams don't attract big people." David Lloyd George, the former Prime Minister of England, once said, "Don't be afraid to take a big step if one is indicated. You can't cross a chasm with two small steps." Don't be afraid to take a risk if the right opportunity comes along.

Now I want to say a word to your wife, and then I am going to talk to your team leaders. You may want to listen in.

A Word to the Pastor's Wife

Team Seven is the pastor's wife's friend. In the past, each day of his ministry took a little more of him from you and the family. Team Seven clones your husband and gives him back to you a little at a time.

It's like Team Seven makes the time warp go in reverse. Your evenings can now be spent together because he can now spend a portion of his day in the coffee shop instead of every evening out visiting. But more than that, he has others out doing what he taught them. Doesn't that sound good?

When I developed the Team Seven concept for the business world, more than any other group, wives thanked me for the fact that now they and their husbands could build their organizations in the day and have their evenings free to

go to the symphony, the ball games, or just stay home if they
wanted to.

I hope it works out that way for you, too. I believe it will.
Now I need to talk to the team leaders from your church. I
would like to invite you and your husband to sit in.

Before they get here, just a word of caution to you, pastor.
You will make a mistake from which you may never recover
if you appoint your team leaders. Make them earn the title.
A team leader is one who has gone out and built a team of
seven new church members. He has earned the right to the
position. Let everyone earn their positions in Team Seven.

You and I offer the opportunity to anyone who wants to
begin to put a team together. We must not appoint someone
to a title which others have to earn. That only breeds contempt for the one appointed and the one who appointed him.

15

A Word to the Team Leader

I sit down alone,
    Only God is here;
In his presence I open,
    I read his books;
And what I thus learn,
    I teach.
            —John Wesley

This is your chance. You may have been active in the church all your life, or you may have never done anything for the Lord. Maybe you've wanted to do something special that did not depend on what the rest of the membership did. You wanted something where no one could hold you back. Maybe you wanted something you could use to get your Sunday School class or department going, or your campus ministry. Maybe this is it.

With Team Seven, you as a member can go about your networking the kingdom regardless of what anyone else does or doesn't do. Of course you should always check with your pastor and staff. I am just saying that you can personally minister whether you are in the midst of an old, dead church or a live, vibrant one. You can now have a vibrant witness within any situation.

Many Just Watch the Parade Go By

Many church members never get involved because they have no vehicle. Some wouldn't if the vehicle were a Rolls Royce. Others see an Edsel and think it's a Rolls Royce. They fall for any vehicle or personality. Many just watch the parade go by.

One day I heard a speaker tell a story by Leo Presley about a young boy during the Depression years. The boy heard that the circus was coming to town. He asked his dad for fifty cents for the circus.

His dad responded, "Son, we don't have fifty cents. These are hard times."

The boy was disappointed but worked extra hard on his chores that week. If wood were needed for the fire, he jumped up and ran for it. By the end of the week, his desire and positive attitude had affected his dad. So, as daddies can be known to do, he found the money somewhere for the circus.

That Saturday afternoon the boy ran all the way to town. As he got nearer, he could hear the music. He ran faster. Soon he saw the band. The crowd had gathered along the streets. Like any little boy, he pushed between the crowd and got down on his knees.

First came the band with its instruments and twirlers. Then came the caged animals on trucks with bars. Next came the horses with the trick riders. Along came the clowns doing their jests and somersaults.

One of the clowns did a flip and landed right in front of the little boy and bowed, holding out his hat. The little boy tossed his fifty cents into the hat, and the clown went dancing on down the street followed by the elephants.

As the crowd dispersed, the little boy stood up from his

knees and went home. He said, "It wasn't until years later, as a grown man, that I realized that I had never been to the circus. I had only watched the parade go by."

What a sad and beautiful story. It reminds me of so many church members. They never get involved in anything. They just watch the parade go by.

Team Seven is your chance to go to the circus.

Some Will Help and Some Won't

There was a certain man who had two sons. He went to the first son and said, 'Son, go and work today in my vineyard.'

The son answered, 'I will not go.' But later the son decided he should go, and he went.

Then the father went to the other son and said, 'Son, go and work today in my vineyard.' The son answered, 'Yes, sir, I will go and work.' But he did not go.

—Matthew 21:28–31

As you begin training your team members to become future team leaders, you will soon discover something your pastor and staff have known all along. Not everyone who says, "I will help you," does. Not everyone who says, "I will not help you," doesn't. You ask everyone, but you will drive yourself crazy trying to sit around and think who will and who won't, and why.

Have a Smile Class

A man that hath friends must shew himself friendly.
—Proverbs 18:24 (King James Version)

You may also find that you need to have a "Smile" class or a "How to Be Happy Looking" class. One of the first things your team members need to learn is how to be positive. Recommend a copy of Dr. Schuller's book *Possibility Thinking,* or one of Dr. Peale's, or Dale Carnegie's. Mother Teresa said:

Some people came to Calcutta, and before leaving, they begged me: "Tell us something that will help us to live our lives better." And I said: "Smile at each other; smile at your wife, smile at your husband, smile at your children, smile at each other—it doesn't matter who it is—and that will help you to grow up in greater love for each other."[1]

Right off the bat, you can say to them, "Tell your face to be happy." Fred Waring used to say, "I can stand in another room and listen to the Pennsylvanians sing and tell if they are smiling."

Some people look like they went to Comatose State and didn't graduate. Sometimes they think they are smiling, but their faces don't show it. Most people can't read our minds. We need to "Show ourselves friendly." So get your smile class started. My son, Chris, was describing one of his distributors to me, and said, "He looked like he'd chewed the sugar out of his gum."

Have you ever heard anyone say, "I went to that church and they weren't friendly?" Or perhaps, "I went to that church and didn't meet one friend." Or this, "No one spoke to me."

It takes so little for us to smile and say, "Hello." Why is it so hard for us? I don't know but sometimes it is, though, isn't it? I heard a preacher use this poem one day. It says so much:

> I went out to find a friend,
>   And there was no one there.
> I went out to be a friend,
>   And friends were everywhere.

A Rose Petal Smells Best After It Has Been Crushed

Devils can be driven out of the heart by the touch of a hand on a hand or a mouth.[2]

—Tennessee Williams

It is not enough to be an effective team leader. Your training is not finished until you have learned how to teach what you know to someone else, and you have done that.

How do you spot a potential team leader? First of all, a person may not look or act like a team leader prior to your recruiting and training him.

Offer the opportunity to everyone. But your job will be half complete if you go after potential team leaders who already have people skills. But don't exclude anyone.

Sometimes, someone will say, "But he is too important, or he has too high a position. I could never talk to him."

God can use the "up and out" as well as the "down and out." I tell my associates, "It doesn't matter if he is the Sergeant at Arms for the P.T.A., or has diamonds on the soles of his shoes, offer him a chance. Otherwise, you play God, and make his decision for him. If he doesn't want help, let him tell you. The word will get back to God. He'll find out."

Even "trust babies" should be offered the chance. They are usually anxious to take on anything that helps them shake off the "golden handcuffs."

What I am saying is, "Don't overlook anyone just because of his position in life, whether it is high or low." When God came to find me, I was getting my toys out of the city dump, and hiding in the school outhouse eating the scraps I had picked up for my teacher's dog. We were so poor that the church mouse stayed at our house. So when looking for team leaders, don't overlook people who are where I was, or am.

Let me mention one other group you might pay special attention to when looking for a team leader. The church is full of people who have been broken for one reason or another. These people are very teachable. They don't have to be taught how to care or the importance of bonding. They thrive on it. Don't forget: Other than spiritual reasons, there are only two reasons a person will not succeed as a team leader:

1. He or she cannot handle it emotionally, or

2. He or she is not teachable.

My physician friends tell me that a bone that has been broken grows back stronger where the break was.

A rose looks so beautiful and smells so good sitting in a vase. But its best fragrance is produced after the petals have been crushed. Some people do their best work for God after they have been crushed.

Broken people make good team leaders, too. Who among us hasn't stepped in a pothole or two? Sometimes you have to help them know that God has forgiven them, or He has restored them, or He has a plan. You have to help them to accept the situation and go on and not keep carrying the guilt or burden. Simon Tugwell tells the story of two monks in Japan:

> . . . traveling together down a muddy road. A heavy rain was still falling. Coming around a bend, they met a lovely girl in a silk kimono and sash, unable to cross the intersection. "Come on, girl," said Tanzan at once. Lifting her in his arms, he carried her over the mud. Ekido did not speak again until that night when they reached a lodging temple. Then he no longer could restrain himself. "We monks don't go near females," he told Tanzan, "especially not young and lovely ones. It is dangerous. Why did you do that?" "I left the girl there," said Tanzan. "Are you still carrying her?"

Mr. Tugwell then said, "We must learn to pass through situations like a fish, rather than carrying them all with us like a snail."[3]

Attitude Dependable

Any fact facing us is not as important as our attitude toward it, for that determines our success or failure.
          —Norman Vincent Peale

Other than the spiritual qualities in a leader, I would rather have a team leader with a good attitude than almost any other quality. I look for people who are attitude dependable. Let me illustrate.

At the same university, different years, I had two students with almost equal talent. One's name was Cynthia, and let's call the other student Sue in order to protect the innocent.

We'd been there all week at the studio in Hollywood, doing a show for National TV for the Wendell Niles Studio and the Colgate Palmolive Company. My group was the Heritage Singers. The head of the production was also a top executive for one of the major TV networks.

I said, "Bob, I have this little red-headed girl I want you to hear while we are out here."

He said, "Love to. Catch me in between sessions, and I'll do it."

Every day I would watch for a time when I could get him to sit down long enough to listen to her. She was on standby, just in case. She never complained, nor acted frustrated. When he couldn't be there, she just smiled and bounced off to be with the rest of the group.

Finally I said, "Bob, we're going home tomorrow. I want you to hear this girl. I told her you would. I can't let her down."

He said, "Bring her at lunch. I'm brown-bagging it today anyway." We did. He sat there on a prop box and ate as he listened to her. He liked her.

Two years later, same situation, except we only had one day. My group was auditioning at C.B.S. Studios for another show. Before the audition I said, "Bob, I've got another student here I'd like for you to listen to when we get through."

Same response. "O.K. Love to. Just catch me when we get through with your group."

After the audition, I introduced him, and said, "This is Sue, the singer I wanted you to hear."

Bob said, "Gotta run. Catch you later."

I knew what he meant. But Sue, who had a hot temper, blew up, pitched a fit, and went out and sat on the bus and pouted.

The rest of us walked across the street to the Farmers' Market and sat down to eat lunch. Guess who walked in.

The C.B.S. executive walked over and said, "May I sit with you? Where is that singer I am supposed to hear?"

I didn't have the heart to tell him about the tantrum. I just said, "Sue's not here." I no longer wanted to recommend the student. You see, it wasn't just the voice I was recommending, but also the attitude.

I don't know what ever happened to Sue.

But Cynthia was on national TV six times during her junior and senior years in college. She appeared on the Lawrence Welk Show several times, the Arthur Godfrey Show, the Dionne Warwick Show, and the summer replacement for the Carol Burnett Show. She later went on to win the Dove Award more than once. You may have heard of her. Her name is Cynthia Clawson, first lady of Christian music.

Often our attitude depends upon whether we are "pitching or catching," doesn't it? Looking at the "Bridge of Sighs," our response depends upon our viewpoint. If we are inside, looking out on the city of Venice for the last time before being thrown into the dungeon, we might respond with a sigh, too. But if we are looking at it as a tourist, from a gondola, we respond with a smile and say, "Look at that!"

But here I am talking about life situations that affect our attitudes. Does attitude make a difference? I was having lunch with a man in Austin, Texas. He told me that as a young salesman, on the road, just getting started, he only had enough money to call home once a week to check on his wife and children. He said he usually slept on a bench at a bus station. That'll check your attitude.

He could have become bitter during this time, but he told me that that was when he was developing his "Laws of Leadership." These "Laws" became the foundation of his book, *Life Is Tremendous,* which sold over a million copies. His name: Charlie "Tremendous" Jones.

Does attitude make a difference? You handle it from here. I look for potential team leaders with a good attitude.

Persistence and Consistency

If you can wait and not be tired by waiting . . .
                    —Rudyard Kipling

Another quality I look for when trying to find a potential team leader is persistence. I am not talking about hounding people to death down at the office where you work, and leaving the impression you are a religious freak of some sort. Those people are about as useful in kingdom networking as a stewardess on a helicopter or a screen door on a submarine.

We say, "Use pleasant persistence and good judgment." If a person was a know-it-all in traditional witnessing, Team Seven will not make him less a know-it-all.

Other than the spiritual aspects of networking the kingdom, persistence and consistency stand at the top of the qualities needed in a leader.

> Nothing in the world can take
> the place of persistence . . .
> Talent will not; nothing is more
> common than unsuccessful
> men with talent. . . .
> Genius will not; unrewarded
> genius is almost a proverb.
> Education will not; the world
> is full of educated derelicts.
> Persistence and determination
> alone are omnipotent. The
> slogan "press on" has solved,
> and always will solve, the
> problems of the human race.
>   —Calvin Coolidge

Chris, my youngest son, came home from church camp one summer and told me the best illustration on persistence and consistency I have heard to this day.

The speaker told the story of an experiment someone had

done. A steel beam was tied to a metal cable and hung from the ceiling of a building. They roped off the area so no one would get hurt.

Using only the forefinger, someone tapped lightly on the steel beam. Some laughed as they watched. The person never did more than tap the steel. It of course did not move. By the end of the first hour, the steel beam could be seen to move ever so slightly, if you watched closely.

The beam never received more than a gentle tap. An hour later, the beam was beginning to swing a little more. Still the man gently tapped.

By the end of the day, from the gentle, consistent tapping of the forefinger, the steel beam was swinging from one end of the building to the other.

All it takes to get some people to consider coming into the kingdom is a gentle tap. But often the tap has to come over and over. Og Mandino put it this way:

> I will persist until I succeed.
>
> I was not delivered into this world in defeat, nor does failure course in my veins. I am not a sheep waiting to be prodded by my shepherd. I am a lion and I refuse to talk, to walk, to sleep with the sheep.
>
> The slaughter house of failure is not my destiny.
>
> I will persist until I succeed.[4]

The Ten-Cow Wife

As a team leader, you probably already know that your people will respond to your leadership in accordance with how they think you feel about them. That's amazing, isn't it? That's why we must constantly be saying to our team members, "You can do it. I know you can do it. I believe in you."

Let me illustrate how important this is. The story is not original.

As was the custom, a very wise man had picked out his future wife and went to her father to make arrangements as to what dowry the father expected for his daughter.

The father said, "For my daughter, ten chickens."

The future husband said, "I'll give you ten cows."

"Agreed."

Five years later, same scene.

The father said, "Why did you pay me ten cows when you could have had my daughter for ten chickens? You are supposed to be a very wise man."

The husband replied, "I paid you ten cows instead of ten chickens because I wanted a ten-cow wife. I wanted her to know forever that she was a ten-cow wife and not a ten-chicken wife. I made a good decision. Now she thinks she is a ten-cow wife."

It is important that our team members know that we think they are ten-cow team members instead of ten-chicken team members.

Managers Instruct; Leaders Inspire

Leadership is "the art of getting someone else to do something that you want done because he wants to do it."
—Dwight D. Eisenhower

In picking future team leaders, watch out for those who want to manage. What you want are those who can inspire their team members.

In seeking team leaders, use your best judgment and common sense, but let God do the picking. I don't know what it is, but "He specializes in things that seem impossible." He made a donkey talk once.

A team member may say to you, "I could never be the kind of team leader you are. I just couldn't do that."

I say, "Does it look to you like I know how to be a pretty good team leader?"

He says, "Sure, but I could never do that."

I say, "If I am already doing pretty well, if you and I teamed up, couldn't we do better?"

He says, "Oh, sure. I could do it if you went with me."

I say, "I'm going with you until we get your team seven deep. Longer if I need to."

In our haste to build a great and large church, let's not overlook the shy and those who appear to have no obvious talent for networking the kingdom. What surprises often come our way.

Evidently someone had this same conversation with Saint Francis of Assisi. In response to why God was using him in such a way, he said:

This may be why: The Lord looked down from Heaven and said, "Where can I find the weakest, littlest man on earth?" Then He saw me and said, "I've found him. I will work through him, and he won't be proud of it. He'll see that I am only using him because of his insignificance."[5]

Be careful to offer the opportunity to everyone. How could God help but respond to the prayer of the helpless?

> When other helpers fail,
> And comforts flee,
> Help of the helpless,
> O abide with me![6]

Chapter 12 is entitled "Transferring Leadership." It's for everybody, but especially for you. Now, if you'll excuse me a minute, I need to move over to another booth and talk to one of your new team members. See you later. Or you may sit in on it.

Remember, though, your primary responsibility is to make sure all of the team members make it. Robert Swan was the first man ever to walk to both the North Pole and the South Pole. Someone asked him, "What was the hardest part of the ice walk to the North Pole?" He replied: "Making sure the rest of the team got there, too."

16

A Word to the New Team Member

Everyone has inside of him a piece of good news. The good news is that you don't know how great you can be! How much you can love! What you can accomplish! And what your potential is!

—Anne Frank

Well, you've done it. You've decided to join us and make a run at this thing called Team Seven, and someone shoved a copy of this book into your hands and said, "Teach yourself."

We'll try to talk you through the deal. You don't know it now, but you are pretty important to us. You see, you are the whole reason for the concept of networking the kingdom. You are the result of our networking the kingdom.

As you begin with us, let's make it an adventure and have fun. Could we agree that we won't take ourselves too seriously and that we won't be too dogmatic in our teaching? Let's learn together.

The person who recruited you to be a team member, or

your team leader, will have the responsibility of training you and showing you around the church and its activities. If that person becomes inactive, or you can't work with him, go upline to the pastor or a staff member. We don't want you to get lost in the cracks.

I'm going to tell you what a very important and pretty lady told me when she and her husband introduced me to networking. Since then I've taught the saying to all my associates. I want to pass it on to you. The reason it is so important is so that you can begin weaning yourself immediately from your team leader. Your goal should be to become your own team leader. This statement will get you started. Here it is:

> If it is to be,
> it's up to me.

Promise me you won't forget it, and that you will teach it to all your new team members. Promise? Good. One of our all-time greatest generals said it another way. He said:

Accept the challenges, so that you may feel the exhilaration of victory.

—General George S. Patton

Team Seven is a tool, similar to a piece of equipment. If you don't use it, it's of little value to you. A boat in dry dock is of little use to a fisherman.

God provided the tool. He expects us to provide what we call in real estate "sweat equity." As Carlo Carretto says:

God gives us the boat and the oars, but then tells us, "It's up to you to row." Making "positive acts of faith" is like training this faculty; it is developed by training, as the muscles are developed by gymnastics.[1]

You understand that we, those who were already church members when you joined us, have feet of clay. Your example should be Jesus and not us, because sometimes when we are tired, we may be short with you, or we may appear lazy or indifferent. We don't mean to. We always want you to think the best of us, but we are not always at our best.

The Difference Between Horses and Donkeys

As you get to know us better, you will come to understand that we have two kinds of church members. I don't know how to describe this, but there are definitely two kinds. I am going to tell you a story that I heard a preacher tell one time; you apply it.

Mountain lions usually don't prey on domestic livestock. But sometimes when they don't have enough to eat, they come down and attack the horses and donkeys.

When the horses sense the danger, they gather in a circle and put their heads together facing in, and their hind feet pointed out toward the danger. As a team, they kick and kick at the mountain lion until the danger passes.

When the donkeys sense the same danger, they gather in a circle with their hind legs facing in and their heads facing out toward the danger. They bray and bray and kick each other.

That is a little bit of information that may come in handy some day. If you are in a situation at the church that is uncomfortable, just notice whether the members are kicking the problem or each other.

I hope you don't ever need that illustration, but I bet you will if you live long enough.

First Things First

As you look at the church bulletin, you probably feel like you are in a maze and don't know which activities you and your family should participate in. You probably feel that if you got in on everything, the first thing you would need to do is join a health club and get in better shape. Something like a marathon.

The activities at most churches are sort of like a cafeteria. You pick and choose. If you ate everything at the cafeteria, you would probably get sick. The staff doesn't want you to join everything either. There is so much because there are so many people who have different needs and interests.

There are some things that are so important that if you plan to grow, you have no choice but to participate. I assume that you have already joined the church and are attending. Otherwise, you wouldn't already be a team member.

The second thing you need to do is to attend the first four Sundays of the class for new members, if your new church offers this. If it doesn't, don't attend that class. Stay with me, now.

I think the next most important thing is for you to attend a Sunday School or Bible School class on Sunday morning. If you have gotten that far, you are pretty well plugged into the main activities of the church. All other events are usually announced at one of these activities.

All of the important doctrines of our faith are taught there. That may not seem as important to you as the fact that in Sunday School we are also taught how to live in this crazy, mixed-up world. Most importantly, we are taught how to get along with each other.

Robert Fulghum, in a poem from his best-seller book by the same name; *All I Really Need to Know I Learned in Kindergarten,* says it pretty well:

Most of what I really need to know about how to live and what to do and how to be I learned in kindergarten. Wisdom was not at the top of the graduate school mountain, but there in the sandpile at Sunday School. These are the things I learned:

Share everything.
Play fair.
Don't hit people.
Put things back where you found them.
Clean up your own mess.

Don't take things that aren't yours.
Say you're sorry when you hurt somebody.
Wash your hands before you eat.
Flush.
Warm cookies and cold milk are good for you.
Live a balanced life—learn some and think some and
    draw and paint and sing and dance and play and
    work every day some.
Take a nap every afternoon.
When you go out into the world, watch out for traffic,
    hold hands and stick together.
Be aware of wonder.[2]

Master the Ten Steps to Networking the Kingdom

The next thing for you to do is to master the Ten Steps to Networking the Kingdom. Go over them with your sponsor, the one who recruited you. Be sure you have listened to your first six tapes. After doing this, you need to go to work on getting your first team seven deep. We want you to become a team leader. That way, we can clone ourselves. If we teach you to do this, you can clone yourself.

Remember, it is not enough for you to recruit people and dump them. Otherwise, we cannot harvest their networks. Your responsibility, after you have recruited someone, is to teach and bond. Teach your new team members everything you were taught, and bond with them individually so each one feels welcome and cared for.

Make your friend feel so special that he will want to say to his network of friends, "Come and see this special place and these special people. I have found the church I have been looking for all of my life."

There is one thing that I didn't tell your pastor and your team leader. I didn't tell them because I want you to tell them. Go to the pastor or your team leader and say something like this, "Pastor, since we have all these new members, I know it's hard for you and all the other members to remember the names of those of us who are new. You can imagine how hard it is for us to remember the names of all of you who have had years to remember each others' names. Do you think it would be all right, for a few Sundays, if we had name tags for at least some of the activities? We like the way you make us feel special by calling us by our names."

If the pastor won't adopt your suggestion about name tags, I know how you can get him to remember your name. Go build a team of seven in two weeks. He'll remember your name, and probably everyone else in history will, too.

Do you know how many church members have gone out and personally brought in seven new members in two weeks? Very few. In fact, it may never have been done. I've always been one who liked to do things that have never been done. How about you?

It's all right if you only get *one* new member on your team your first two weeks. But wonder who that first person in history will be who gets seven? I'm not talking about preachers and revivals. I'm talking about you, a new church member. Wow! I wish I were a new member.

I Can Read Your Mind

I have a game that I play with small children. I say, "I can read your mind." Then I take out a pen and paper, and without them seeing what I write, I write down the number 3. I then fold the paper up as small as it will go. I hand it to the youngster or his brother, and tell him to hold it while he answers a question about what I have written on the paper.

I then say, "Say out loud a number between one and five." Most of the time the child yells out, "Three." I then say, "Open the paper and read the answer." In shock they look at me, and sometimes even their parents are careful what they think around me the rest of the time. If the child answers with another number than three, I ask his brother what number he was thinking of and tell them I must have read the wrong mind. They have to be real young, though.

Now I am going to tell you one of the most important things I will say to you. In fact, it is so personal that you will think I read your mind. I don't mean to embarrass you, and if this is a little too close for us to get, since we hardly know each other, tell me, and I'll try to do better in my next writing.

Here it is. I know what you are thinking about networking the kingdom, for the same reason I knew the child's number was three, and with the same odds. Most of the time.

You are probably thinking, "I am not good enough to be bringing anyone else into the kingdom. You don't know my background." You say, "Let me become good enough, or at least get used to the new me, going to church and all, before I begin a Team Seven effort."

Got pretty close, didn't I? Do you know why? Because the rest of us think we aren't good enough, either. Even those of us who have not taken a leave of absence from the church feel that way. Wonder why that is?

I bet the Devil has something to do with it. You know, he likes to whip us over the head with our past. Sometimes we probably need it, but let's let the Lord whip us, and not the Devil. At least the Lord chastens us with love. Few of us feel worthy. And most of those who do, aren't very.

In summary, all of networking the kingdom falls on your shoulders. If you don't do it, it won't get done. Your team leader, under the guidance of the pastor, will do his part, but you are the one on the front line. I leave you with this illustration:

Fred Somebody, Thomas Everybody, Pete Anybody and Joe Nobody were neighbors, but they were not like you and me. They were odd people and most difficult to understand. The way they lived was a shame. All four belonged to the same church but you couldn't have enjoyed worshipping with them. *Everybody* went fishing on Sunday or stayed home to visit with friends. *Anybody* wanted to worship but was afraid *Somebody* wouldn't speak to him so *Nobody* went to church. Really, *Nobody* was the only

decent one of the four. *Nobody* did the visitation. *Nobody*
worked on the church building. Once they needed a Sunday School teacher. *Everybody* thought *Somebody* would
teach. Guess who finally did it? That's right . . . *Nobody!*

It happened that a fifth neighbor (an unbeliever) came to
live among them. *Everybody* thought *Somebody* should try
to win him. *Anybody* could have at least made an effort. But
guess who finally won him to Christ?

That's right . . . *Nobody!*

17

How Should I Present Team Seven to My Church?

Can you think of anything more permanently elating than to know that you are on the right road at last?
—Vernon Howard

An often-asked question is, "How should I present the Team Seven concept to my church or group?" Don't.

It is a skill to be learned, not a program to be adopted. The concept is too new to be presented first to a large group. It is my recommendation that you introduce it to your staff, one at a time, and then to some of your key people, whom you wish to involve in this project. Present it to them one at a time, or at most two at a time. Get them a copy of *Networking the Kingdom* and the first six tapes. Let the book and tapes do your work for you before you even meet with them.

The Team Seven concept is enthusiastically embraced 99.9 percent of the time when first presented one on one. But when first presented to a group, only 70 percent of the group respond favorably immediately. Why?

When someone sews a patch over a hole in an old coat, he
never uses a piece of cloth that is not yet shrunk. If he does,
the patch will shrink and pull away from the coat. Then the
hole will be worse.

Also, people never pour new wine into old leather bags
for holding wine. If they do, the old bags will break. . . .
But people always pour new wine into new wine bags.

—Matthew 9:16–17

I jumped up and down when Ralph, my brother, found
this verse for me. I knew it, but had not thought of it for
here. Jesus had already told us not to mix the old and the
new. My common sense and experience had taught me that,
but it was nice to have it confirmed.

Your common sense, or my experience, had better tell
you that, too. Or, you are going to "split some old garments"
and you and I know whose garments are going to get split,
don't we?

If you're going to slide down a bank, you want to know
where the cactus is. I'm telling you where the cactus is.

Jesus does not say that the old is better than the new, nor
vice versa. He just says, "Don't mix them."

Why not mix them? Team Seven is so foreign to most
people's thinking that you will need time to sell them on
the idea. You can't just present it, and hope the idea will
sell itself.

Some brother or sister might think, "I know my church;
they'll do anything I recommend." In their excitement
they run in to the deacon's meeting, or business meeting,
and start spouting off about Team Seven and doubling
the size of the church and Coffee Shop Meetings, and
. . . . and. . . .

They'll run out about as fast as they ran in. That is not
the way to present it. Forewarned is forearmed. Most people will do it their way anyway, but I felt I ought to say this.

Charles Browner has this to say about new ideas:

A new idea is delicate. It can be killed by a sneer or a yawn;
it can be stabbed to death by a quip and worried to death by
a frown on the right man's brow.[1]

Most People and Churches Are Where They Are Because That's Where They Want to Be

The road winds up the hill to meet the height;
  Beyond the locust hedge it curves from sight—
And yet no man would foolishly contend
  That where he sees it not, it makes an end.
                                    —Emma Carleton

Some of those with whom you talk will have honest, sincere concerns and questions. You should welcome those. It doesn't mean that they are against the concept; they just have questions. Welcome those.

But then there are those who are born in the objective case and live in the kickative mood. They are against anything new. We have to love the lambs as well as the old butting rams.

In any congregation or group you have those who aren't for or against anything. They, too, have their place.

There is a group in any congregation that is very comfortable with their fellowship as it exists. Anything that threatens that fellowship is frowned upon.

Then there are the traditionalists. "It never was done that way here before." We want to love tradition, but try not to become traditionalists.

Beware of one type of member. That is the frustrated individual, for whatever the reason, who desires a platform for his hidden agenda. Listen to him in private, but don't give him a platform.

Determine If the Church Truly Wants to Grow

Faith—is the Pierless Bridge
Supporting what We see
Unto the Scene that We do not—
                          —Emily Dickinson

What a funny comment. Not so. I've talked with staff members who said, "Are you kidding? Where do you think they'd park?"

I was helping with the choir program at a church one time. The choir loft got full. We talked to the deacons, asking if they would consider expanding the choir loft. One deacon actually said, "Maybe the attendance will fall off and we won't have to."

Find those who are like-minded and who want to grow. Find someone who believes in you, and to whom you make sense. If you can't find one person like this, you're in trouble or in the wrong place. Take those people into your confidence, and make them promise they won't begin talking about the concept until you tell them they can. Go do it, and don't talk it to death.

Why should they not go around the church talking about the concept? Many who receive the explanation from an untrained person will misjudge it as a new program for the church to adopt, instead of a technique of church growth to be adapted to the current program. The new person doesn't know what to say and what not to say. If they go out and begin spouting off about how it works, and a neighbor puts them down or pours cold water on the concept, you may have to pour some cold water on them to revive them.

Tell your team leaders, "If you want to do something, read the book, listen to your six tapes, and go to networking. But don't go around the church, taking a survey as to what anyone thinks of networking the kingdom."

Allow enough time for your people to digest what you have taught them before asking them to make a commitment to help you. And don't ask them at the end of your first private meeting with them what they think. They don't have enough information to have an opinion at that point. If they have listened to their first six tapes and read *Networking the Kingdom*, they should be ready to give you an opinion.

While you can invite someone to coffee and get them to church in a ten-minute meeting, you need to devote at least an hour to go over this with any new person. Insist that they keep an open mind for a few days while they are digesting it.

We're Down on What We're Not Up On

The average person is down on what he is not up on. Until it is presented to him, and he has been told the whole story, he will probably say something like, "That might work in one of those big Texas churches, but it'll never work here in Sydney, Australia."

The one thing you know you will not hear, at least early in our efforts: "We tried that at our church and it didn't work." That's refreshing.

Any sufficiently advanced technology is indistinguishable from magic.

—Arthur C. Clarke

18
Setting the Goals for You and Your Church

You make up your mind before you start that sacrifice is part of the package.

—Richard M. DeVos

If you decide to use Team Seven in your church or organization, you will need to set the goals you desire to achieve. You need to decide what you are willing to commit to. If you want to double in size in a year, that dictates how many teams you will need. Not as many as you probably think.

I'm a teacher, so humor me a moment. I want you to get out a piece of paper right now. Write down on it what it would take to double the size of your church this year. If that's too earthshaking for you, write down what it would take to double the net increase in talents the church harvested last year.

Got that written down? You don't have to show it to anyone. Now divide that number by twenty-one, and you will know how many team leaders you need to get it done. That assumes that no team leader gets more than seven new families in a year (we're allowing three to a family; $3 \times 7 = 21$ new talents).

You don't need as many as you thought, do you? Now you have the concrete part done, your goal. Just get some leaders and tell them you want them to become team leaders in ninety days. You and the Lord of the Harvest will have doubled the church in ninety days instead of a year.

> Reduce your plan to writing. . . . The moment you complete this, you will have definitely given concrete form to the intangible desire.
>
> —Napoleon Hill

Let me help you a little more. This is fun, isn't it? For figuring purposes, let's say your church has three hundred in it, and you wish to double this year. That would mean you need three hundred new people for a total of six hundred.

Let's assume that the first year a team leader is going to build only one team of seven. Some will do more, some less. But anyone can do this without breaking a sweat.

Now, let's assume that each new team member is a family of an average of three. I think that's the national average.

A team of seven new members with three in each family would be twenty-one new people brought in by each team.

Now our goal is three hundred new people. We divide that by twenty-one to get the number of teams needed: 14.29, rounded off to 15. Could you find 15 people in your church to whom you could sell the concept one on one? Voila. There it is. Your church just doubled.

> March on. Do not tarry. To go forward is to move toward perfection. March on, and fear not the thorns, or the sharp stones on life's path.
>
> —Kahlil Gibran

Don't try to sell the church membership on the deal. Let it come through the individuals, from the bottom up. In a few Sundays, people will start saying, "Where are all these new people coming from?"

Tunnel Vision

Vision. . . . It reaches beyond the thing that is, into the conception of what can be. Imagination gives you the picture. Vision gives you the impulse to make the picture your own.

—Robert Collier

If you decide to make a commitment to yourself, your church, and God, you'll jump in with both feet and get it done, if you are like most leaders I know.

I was talking with the pastor of one large, fast-growing church, and he said, "I've got one leg over the fence. I'm about ready to throw the other over." He did.

I tell my business associates, "When you make a goal, rule out all distractions. Any decisions in your business that need to be made should be preceded by this question, 'Will it get me closer to my goal?'"

If you make a commitment, not a promise, all else will fall by the wayside, I heard a successful networker say one day, "Small dreams don't attract big people." If you make a major commitment, you will burn with zeal, and your spouse and church won't know what happened to you.

The Reticular Activating System (R.A.S.)

Any idea, plan, or purpose may be placed in the mind through repetition of thought.

—Napoleon Hill

I am told by physicians that there is a part of the brain called the "reticular activating system" (R.A.S.). It is that portion of the brain that helps us with goal setting.

I am also told that the verbal portion of the brain is the strongest portion of the brain. That's why businesses, football teams, and everyone else involved in motivating groups, have people write their goals down and say them out loud.

It is of vital importance that you get your people to write

down their goals, and share them verbally with someone who cares.

Many people write their goals down and tape them on their refrigerators.

Let's be careful with this. Just having a goal and being enthusiastic about it is not enough. I have seen people try this, and the first brother-in-law that pokes at them bursts their bubble, and you don't see them around any more. James 2:20 says, "Faith without works is dead." Enthusiasm without works is too. Lazy leaders try to get their people worked up with enthusiasm alone. That's cruel.

Dr. James Dobson tells the story of a high-school football team that had lost all year. They were offered a special prize if they won. They became very enthusiastic but still lost. He says, "Hoorah and whoop-de-do can't compensate for an absence of discipline and conditioning and practice and study and coaching and drill and experience and character."[1]

If you have a goal that you have made a major commitment to, a portion of your brain filters out everything else. For example, a mother is at home asleep. Her baby is asleep in another room. A train goes by, the police sirens blast, there is thundering and lightning, and the TV is going. The mother sleeps through it all.

But let her baby cry out, and she is up and in there in a flash. Wonder why that is? It's because she filtered out all other sounds but the sound of her baby.

Our mind works that way when we set a goal. Even more so if it is bathed in prayer, and you are convinced that God is guiding you. I think you and I would agree, all original thought comes from Him.

The Difference Between Commitment and Involvement

There is a difference between saying, "I'll try it a while," and saying, "I'll commit my whole being to it." Some people just piddle around and sort of get involved.

You want the kind of people as your team leaders who are

made up so that if they make a commitment, the job gets done. You know the kind. You want the ones who will say, "If it isn't done when you come back, you'll find me standing here in a puddle of blood."

The best illustration of the difference between commitment and involvement is the story of the pig and the chicken told by a pastor. He had just had bacon and eggs. He said, "The chicken was involved, but the pig was committed."

We at Networking the Kingdom Headquarters will do our best to match our commitment to yours. Should you desire it, we'll do our part to provide support materials and training for you and your group through our two-day seminars and our Tape Program.

The Automatic Shipment Program of a tape each month keeps you updated on the concept as it develops from different parts of the world. We won't tell everyone, but we'll tell you everything we learn. So, as you have little or big successes as you network the kingdom, let us know. We'll pass the information along.

A New Perspective

> The greatest discovery of my generation is that human beings can alter their lives by altering their attitudes of mind.
> —William James

You decide what goals you want for yourself or your church. Sometimes all we need is for our minds to take just a slightly different twist, and then everything becomes clear. And sometimes we only "see in part." In bridge, the common expression is, "One peek is worth two finesses."

When Frank and Ralph take my boys and me coon hunting in Tennessee, we sometimes get lost. Even the dogs get lost. In the pitch black of those mountains, an instant of sight that comes with a flash of lightning can save your life, if you are about to step off a high bluff.

I tell my networkers that you don't have to be smart all of your life, just about fifteen seconds. "What if you had invented the yo yo?" "What if?" is a good question when your mind won't turn a corner.

Let me illustrate. The engineers were about to dismantle the underpass or the truck. These seemed to be the only two options. The underpass was an inch too short, or the truck was an inch too tall. This too-tall truck had made a sharp turn and started under the too-low bridge. It was stuck. It couldn't back up and couldn't go through.

A little boy came by on his way to a service station, carrying the wheel from his bicycle. Seeing the problem, he pulled on the sleeve of the chief engineer and said, "Why don't you just let the air out of the tires?" So simple. But a new perspective.

That's why your newer members will take to Team Seven like a duck to water, while some of your more "staid" ones will tell you, "You're in over your head," and may try to hold you under for even suggesting such a harebrained idea.

Now, I am going to tell you three stories about beds, and how a new perspective is applied.

First story. I heard about a man who was having trouble sleeping. When he was in his bed, he thought someone was under it. He would look under it, and think someone was in the bed. In it, under it. It was about to drive him crazy.

He went to see a psychiatrist and explained his problem. The doctor said, "I think I can solve your problem, but it will take a session a week at fifty dollars a session, for three years."

The man said, "Let me think about it."

The man saw his psychiatrist three weeks later at their health club. The psychiatrist said, "How did your problem work out about imagining that someone was under your bed and in it?"

"I solved it."

"How?"

"I was telling my problem to my bartender, and he said, 'Why don't you cut the legs off your bed?'"

New perspective.

Second story. Let me show you how our minds trick us.

Now I am telling you in the beginning this is a trick question. Even knowing this, your mind will not compute the solution until I put a "crack of light" in for you.

Here it is: What can you sit in, sleep on, and brush your teeth with? Give up? I did too.

It's a chair, a bed, and a toothbrush.

You say, "But I thought you meant one thing."

But the question didn't say "one thing"; your mind did. Wonder if we could have misjudged some other opportunity, person, or event because of that? All of us do it, don't we?

Most of us bring our own hidden agenda to the opportunity until the "crack of light" breaks through. Sometimes we huff and puff and go on so much that we blow the "crack of light" out.

My third bed story is about the Procrustean Bed. Some will try to force a solution when there is none. Sometimes we just have to live with a situation.

In Eleusis, there lived a giant robber by the name of Procrustes, according to Greek legend. He lured travelers to his house, supposedly to entertain them. He forced them to lie down on an iron bed. If they were too long, he chopped off their legs to fit the bed. If they were too short, he stretched their legs to fit the bed.

He got his comeuppance though. Theseus fitted him to the same bed.

Sometimes even a new perspective is not the answer either. Is it?

Desperate circumstances sometimes bring forth very creative solutions. Bernard Baruch told the story of a man who was sentenced to die. He was negotiating for his life before the king.

The condemned man said to the king, "If you will give me a year before carrying out my sentence, I will teach your horse to fly. If I am successful, I get to go free."

The king agreed.

A friend of the condemned man said to him, "You know you can't teach the king's horse to fly. Why did you do that?"

"That gives me many options. During the year, the king

may die. I may die. Or the horse may die. Who knows? During the year, the horse may learn to fly."

*Set Your Goal in Concrete
But the Date in Sand*

You can plant a dream.
—Anne Campbell

Let's say that you and some of your leaders decide that you want the first period of Team Seven to last for ninety days. At the end of that time, the goal is for each team leader to have seven new church members (a family counts as one) on his or her team.

Question. Is the goal ninety days, or is the goal to get seven new church members on each team? Set the goal of seven new members in concrete. Don't change that. If you don't have it done in ninety days, move the date. It was set in sand.

Why put a time limit on it at all then? Tomorrow will steal Team Seven from you. Unless there is a time limit placed, there is no urgency. Without the clock, a football or basketball game loses its urgency and significance. If we have a year to get seven new team members, we think, "What's the rush, man?"

My recommendation is that you do your big pushes in ninety-day increments. These are easily managed, and are not so far off that we lose the sense of future gratification of our goal.

Go for the Singles, Not the Home Run

When you set your goal, break it down into bite-sized pieces. Don't let your people talk their goal to death. Don't give them a platform for what they are going to do. Only recognize them for what they do.

Everybody thinks networking is a "piece of cake" until they get to doing it. Networking will challenge you at every strength and weakness you have. Your team members will be getting up saying, "I'm in for life." One of my upline sponsors, whose network spans the globe, says, "In a couple of months they are trying to fake death."

"I'm going to get a hundred the first month," they say. You don't want to discourage them, but my comment is, "Just bring me one, and I'll be happy." If we can get one, we can get more.

I have found that networking is not made up of home runs or even doubles. For the most part it is a lot of strike-outs and singles with a few bunts thrown in. Not much of a display case for those who will only be satisfied with home runs. In spite of this, it's possible to build a gigantic network in a relatively short time because of the cloning effect and the geometric progression.

People ask me, "Doesn't your team leader want his or her strongest person at the head of the team?"

I answer, "Not necessarily so. Ever played baseball? Where do you want your clean-up batter? Fourth. Four runs score. If you could have a clean-up batter seventh, seven people would score." By scoring, I'm meaning the team gets seven deep fast.

The Little Bugs Played the Big Bugs

I heard someone tell this story one time. It was half-time and the Big Bugs were ahead 30 to 0. When the game ended, the score was 37 to 30 in favor of the Little Bugs.

One of the Big Bugs asked one of the Little Bugs, "Who was that bug that ran all those touchdowns in the second half?"

The Little Bug said, "Oh, that was Joe Caterpillar."

The Big Bug said, "Where was he during the first half?"

The Little Bug said, "He was tying his shoes."

You will have team members who will analyze the situation to death. It's called "paralysis of analysis." They wait until the game is half over before they get their "shoes tied." Often by then the team has taken the ball and gone home.

If You've Got to Eat a Frog,
the Sooner You Eat it, the Better

I don't know what it is, but once you set a goal, look out. You will be challenged. I don't know where the challenges will come from, but you will be challenged. You just handle the problems as they come up. One of your key team leaders will get a divorce. Someone will lose a job. Someone, whom you just knew was going to be your next superstar in networking, won't even return your calls.

Things will just come up. But you know all that already. That's just life, except that it seems that things matter so much more when you set a goal. You know what I think? I think it must make the Devil mad, and he goes about trying to throw a monkey wrench into things. Now that's not very theological sounding, but I think that's what happens. What do you think?

When things come up, you solve them, and go on. I heard someone say one time, "If you've got to eat a frog, the sooner you eat it, the better. If you've got to eat several frogs, eat the biggest one first."

Keep the path to your goal as clear of all obstacles as you can. Find a solution.

Two deer hunters were sitting in front of their campfire drinking their first cup of coffee of the morning. Both were disgruntled and expressing deep resentment toward their buddy who was still asleep in the camper.

One said, "I'm not coming back next year. I can't sleep with him snoring all night like he does, and I won't go a week without a good night's sleep again."

The second hunter said, "I've got it. Next year let's bring Joe along with us and bring two campers. We'll let Joe sleep in the camper with snoring Sam."

They did. A year later, same scene. The two hunters were sitting there rested from a good night's sleep, and having their first morning cup of coffee as they laughed at the trick they had pulled on Joe. They were a little nervous because snoring Sam was a big rough cowboy-type, and Joe was bigger and rougher than Sam.

Surprise. Out of the camper came snoring Sam, all disheveled and completely out of sorts. Then out came Joe, as rested as if he had stayed at a hotel.

"Didn't Sam's snoring keep you awake, Joe?" they asked.

Joe said, "Yeah, he started snoring, and as soon as he did, I reached over and gave him a kiss on the cheek, and he stayed awake all night watching me."

Sometimes our solutions are not as funny as what happened to the deer hunters. Occasionally, like the story about the Procrustean Bed, our solutions backfire on us.

Let's agree that we won't be so gullible that we swallow everything. But let's also agree that when a new idea, opportunity, or problem presents itself to us, we'll ask, for a while anyway, "What if?"

I will, if you will.

Is the Prize Worth the Price?

One day I was talking with a gold medalist in rifle shooting. He had just returned from Korea, where he was the trainer for some of the Olympic athletes. I said, "If you could say just one thing about goal setting to a person, athlete or not, what would you say?"

He looked away for a moment, then slowly looked around at me, with the type of intensity only an Olympic athlete can muster, breathed deeply, and said, "Is the prize worth the price?" He repeated it, "Yes sir. I'd ask them, 'Is the prize worth the price?'"

Because I don't know of the battles you have won or lost, I don't know why you would choose the goal you have chosen. But you and God know, and that's enough. I know one thing, if it isn't big enough, you'll never know if God had a part in it, or if you did it all by yourself.

Most battles are won before they are fought.
—*Wall Street Journal,* movie ad

Why don't you go out on a limb? That's where the fruit is. Imagine yourself preaching to that audience of 100,000 in the new worship center that you, all your new team members, and the Lord have built. Imagine them fussing at you saying, "We told you to build it for 200,000. It's already too small."

Winston Churchill said:

The empires of the future are the empires of our minds.

Maybe your dream is just to last the year out until your retirement. You may be so tired that you just want to get that year behind you and get down to the fishing hole for a while with a string tied to your toe. You're saying, "I only have a year left to retirement. My active ministry years are down to one." Oh?

"What if? What if you recruited a bunch of thirty-year-olds to help you network the kingdom?" Your active ministry would have the equivalency of a thirty-year-old. You see, if you feel too old, find some young bucks. You may be too old and too tired to work like they do, but you know more than they do until they get to your age. You'll probably still know more than most of them. Work smart, not hard. Easy for me to say, isn't it?

I bet you never thought of that, and I bet you can do it. I know you can do it. Your spouse wouldn't know what happened to you.

It would get that member off your back, too. You know the one I'm talking about. You can really drive people with Team Seven. Get that guy who has been on your back for the last ten years and help him become a team leader. Go to him and say, "I think you're an exception. I think you can start six teams at once." He'll work himself to death, go on to heaven, or somewhere, and leave you alone.

Let's change our thinking from, "If only" to "What if?"

Where there is no vision, the people perish.
—Proverbs 29:18 (King James Version)

19

What If, Using Team Seven, You Could Pastor the World?

The cities and mansions that people dream of are those in which they finally live. . . .

—Lewis Mumford

What an astounding question. What an astounding thought. Remember, "What the mind of man can conceive and believe, he can achieve," according to Napoleon Hill.

It is my firm belief that God hasn't yet built his largest or greatest churches. But He's going to. They are going to need pastors. Why not help Him build one of them yourself? The hour makes the man. Seize the hour.

I think a lot of us thought that mass evangelism, through the use of television, would get the job done. It did a lot. Look what Billy Graham and other honorable servants of God have done in that medium. Some others didn't fare so well. Responsibility without accountability, in too many cases, left the kingdom doors open to abuse by the Raiders of the Lost Heart.

It may be that God just got sick of the mess, and that's why He is just now revealing Team Seven to His church, if He is.

Isn't it kind of funny? After we spent all of that money on advertisements and promotions. It's like the Lord of the Harvest is saying, "Thank you, but I don't need that kind of help. If it's all right, I'll just use my own assets: My people. My Son has already showed you exactly how to do it. He went out and got Andrew. Andrew went out and got Peter. Then came Philip, who got Nathanael. Go out in teams of two. Fail My way first." It's sort of like He's quoting that commercial we used to see on TV, "Please, I'd rather do it Myself."

I guess that it isn't too theological to suggest that God might get sick. I don't guess He cries either, but I wonder about it sometimes. Do you? I wonder about other things, too. I may not be supposed to, but I do.

One of these days, I'm going to sit down with Him, and I have some other questions I am going to ask. I'm going to ask Him, "Why did Hetty Sue, my little sister, never have a chance?" I'm going to say, "Don't You think my Mother deserved better than what she got down here?"

I might not be supposed to, but if I get the chance, I'm going to ask Him. I'm not going to doubt Him, but I'm going to ask Him. I trust His judgment, but I think I could live with it better if I knew why. Do you ever think about stuff like that? I bet He's got a question or two for me and you, too, don't you?

Team Seven Unlocks the
Shackles on Church Growth

Every man is an impossibility until he is born.
—Ralph Waldo Emerson

If Jesus tarries, I believe that by using Team Seven, we will see church growth in such gigantic proportions that we will look back on today and wonder how we could have gone so slowly.

I believe that Team Seven will cause a quantum leap in church growth and will, through reclamation, catapult the church headlong into the twenty-first century, causing the birth of large numbers of churches the size of which none of us ever dreamed.

You see, Team Seven unlocks the shackles that have bound church growth in the past.

While it is true that your network is out there, intact, waiting for you to contact them, it is also true that they can't contact you. It would be easier for a man who is yet unborn to contact his grandchildren than it would for a future prospect for your church to contact his prospect's network.

You see, it all starts with you. It can't start with them. They are unborn prospects. And yet as soon as you begin a network, it begins to work backwards, through existing relationships, so fast that you will never in your lifetime even see all of your network. Even though they are recorded, you will probably never meet them all. Stay with me.

The Hidden Power of Networking

Man's mind stretched to a new idea never goes back to its original dimensions.
                                                            —Oliver Wendell Holmes

Let me show you the hidden power of networking. On numerous occasions I am invited to a town and ushered into the community center where I am to speak to two or three hundred people. "What's so unusual about that?" Here is what is so unusual. I have never met a person in the audience before, have never been to the town before, yet they are all in my network!

Getting the picture? Still a little fuzzy? Okay, let's see if I can clear it up a little. Have you ever had a member move from your church to another city or state? "What if he or she already knew how to network?"

Without going into all the details, with Team Seven, a pastor could very effectively, with the use of his computer and audio and video cassettes, pastor a network in every town where he has a team leader.

Who placed the present barriers in our minds? Who told us that we can only minister at that one building where our church is located? And who told us that we are not to go past the edges of our "church field"? "What if?"

The barriers are not erected which can say to aspiring talents and industry, "Thus far and no farther."
—Ludwig van Beethoven

We were sitting there high on a mountain, overlooking the city of Acapulco, in one of the city's premier restaurants. I was a dinner guest of my parent company, along with two couples who are stars of stage and screen.

Each couple also has a large networking business, so naturally the subject of networking came up. One of the men said, "I look at networking as a polka-dot scarf," as he held up a scarf to illustrate his point.

We sat there at twilight looking over the beautiful city. The other actor looked out and said, "I look at networking like all those lights coming on down there."

I was sitting there wishing I had something profound to say. So I said, "Man, this is tall cotton." But as I basked in the elegance of the evening, my mind went back to Frog Pond Hollar. I remembered the new shirt Mom made for me. She used what was left over from the rest of the family. It was made from three different flour sacks, and I was so proud of it as I hightailed it out across the sycamore foot log to school.

It was a long time before I understood why those kids on that bus laughed. It bothers me more now than it did then because then I was so proud of that shirt that I would have fought anyone on the bus, including the bus driver, if I had thought they were laughing at anything my Mom had made.

As I look back, I know I must have looked like Speck Roads, the clown on Porter Wagner's show. I would probably have laughed too, but I wouldn't have let me know it.

As I sat there with good friends, in all that luxury, I was thinking, "Boy, if those kids on that bus could see me now!"

As I looked out over the city, my eyes momentarily became misty. My mind then raced to another century, another city, another country, another Networker, who looked out over His city, and how His eyes, for a different reason, must have become a little misty, too. All my ideas were not yet clear about *Networking the Kingdom,* but one piece of the puzzle popped into place then and there:

> Jerusalem, Jerusalem! . . . Many times I wanted to help your people. I wanted to gather them together as a hen gathers her chicks under her wings. But you did not let me.
> —Luke 13:34

If you can pastor a church, you can pastor a city; if you can pastor a city, you can pastor a state; if you can pastor a state, you can pastor a . . .

"Couldn't be done." Oh? Look at what Dr. Paul Yongi Cho has done with cell groups in his church in Seoul, Korea—probably the largest Protestant church in the world, with some 500,000 members.

No matter where I am, when I meet a Korean, I talk to him or her about the networking business I plan to start in Korea someday. I ask, "Have you ever heard of Dr. Cho?" Nine out of ten respond, "He's my pastor. We have a group that gets together here in Dallas to worship, but he's our pastor."

Dr. Cho uses cell groups to give him extra outlets. Team Seven incorporates the small-group idea, works in depth, and builds giant networks with every outlet.

Another example. Look at what Dr. Robert Schuller, pastor of the Crystal Cathedral, has done. People everywhere have benefited from his writings. In a very large sense, he is a world pastor.

You say, "But I can't write like Dr. Schuller." Make a video or audio cassette, and send it throughout your network. If you can preach in your own pulpit, you can preach on video. Make a video of your sermon or teachings, and clone yourself throughout your network. God puts the "preach" in you. Team Seven helps put the network in you. Actually, it pulls the network out of you.

Did I say you had to preach like, or adopt the theologies of, Dr. Cho or Dr. Schuller? No. If you thought I did, you missed the point. My point is, here are two giants in the kingdom who have stretched their church fields to encompass the world.

Your great church pastorate is inside you waiting to be unlocked through your network. You don't need to meet another person to begin. Harvest the contacts you have; then harvest theirs. Has the veil lifted from your eyes yet? If not, stay with me. If it has, dream on, brother or sister.

The ancestor of every action is a thought.
—Ralph Waldo Emerson

You'll Run Like a Man with His Hair on Fire

You will remember that Jesus got His team four deep in two days. But as we read further in the Gospel of John, we notice that He said, "He that believeth on me, the works that I do shall he do also; and greater works than these shall he do; because I go unto my Father" (John 14:12, King James Version).

He got four deep in two days. He said if we believe in Him, we can do "greater works." Perhaps we could get five deep in two days. What do you think? Do you remember?

T E A M

/ Jesus
/ Andrew
/ Peter
/ Philip
/ Nathanael
/ Your Prospect?

Sometimes we are such realists that we can't get the blinders off of our eyes. We are too often like Elisha's servant. Do you remember how he was telling Elisha that the enemy had surrounded them with "horses and chariots"? He was saying, "What are we going to do?" and Elisha was telling him that the Lord's troops were on hand, but he just couldn't see them.

Now put yourself in that servant's shoes. He was probably thinking the same thing your education director may think when you first say to him, "I am going to pastor the world, and I want you to religious education director it. Our network is already intact."

The servant probably thought, and the education director may think, "This dude has been playing hockey with a warped puck."

Can't you just imagine Elisha's servant or the education director pacing nervously back and forth as the enemy got closer and closer? I can hear him as the pitch of his voice got higher and higher, yelling to Elisha, à la Don Knotts, "But I don't see 'em!"

Elisha had what Paul Conn calls "superior information." He knew, as you and I know, that just because the servant couldn't see them, didn't mean they weren't out there. Elisha prayed, and said:

> "Lord, open my servant's eyes. Let him see." The Lord opened the eyes of the young man. And he saw that the mountain was full of horses and chariots of fire all around Elisha.
>
> —2 Kings 6:17

Just because you and I can't see our network doesn't mean it isn't out there. Some have "superior information." We know it's out there, and it's ours to be claimed.

If you've ever dreamed of making your impact on the world in a big way, under the guidance of the Holy Spirit, consider this. With virtually no expense, you can effectively disperse your present ministry into every town where you have a team leader with a network.

Sitting at your computer, you can literally put legs on your prayers, and wings on your dreams, as you call forth reapers to help you reclaim the harvest as you go about networking the kingdom. I can see it now on the sign out in front of your local church: Rev. Joe Network, Pastor of the Great Church.

How high our hopes, how fragile our dreams. Someone said, "The path of least resistance has made every river crooked." Don't let doubt paralyze you. You can do it. I know you can.

If you ever get a hold of the fact that your world network is out there already intact, your Team Seven vehicle is already gassed up with the motor running, and your people are just waiting for you to get there, you'll run like a man with his hair on fire.

Dream lofty dreams, and as you dream, so shall you become. Your vision is the promise of what you shall one day be; your Ideal is the prophecy of what you shall at last unveil.

The greatest achievement was at first and for a time a dream. The oak sleeps in the acorn; the bird waits in the egg; and in the highest vision of the soul a waking angel stirs. Dreams are the seedlings of realities.[1]

Keep me posted. More to come in the next edition.

He who wins the victory will sit with me on my throne.
—Revelation 3:21

20
Geysers and Mud Pots

$\mathbb{W}$ ell, this is where we came in. . . .

We'd just finished lunch and were casually having our second cup of coffee at the Old Faithful Inn. We had plenty of time and were reminiscing over the past week's high points when the forest ranger came running in and announced that the fire was too close. They were going to have to evacuate the Inn. He sent us back out another route to escape the fire that was roaring through the Yellowstone National Park. Before it was over, it would destroy one third of the park.

Ralph, my oldest brother, is the principal of a large elementary school in Tennessee. About a week earlier, when he and I had flown into Jackson Hole to join part of our family for a family reunion, something had appeared wrong with the scenery.

As I told you, I am originally from the Great Smoky Mountains of Tennessee. The smoky look of the Great Smoky Mountains smelled great and refreshing. But there was a smoky look and smell to the mountains of Yellowstone that I had not expected. Somewhere there had to be a fire of significant proportions in the park.

This tour of Yellowstone was sort of like a second childhood for us. More like the first for the one we never had. You would have thought we were the Golden Boys and Girls.

You may remember, we were raised in Frog Pond Hollar, Tennessee. Frog Pond Hollar was not a very forgiving place for children with no shoes, no food, and no floor in the house, and a father who was the town drunk and liked to beat up on little folks.

Some of you have heard me tell my story of how, because of our father's drinking problem, our family was evicted and put out on the street. And how after a few days we wound up in Frog Pond Hollar where the rent was free.

Except for Earlene, Jewell's wife, these are my brothers and sisters. They are the ones I have told you about who as small children had to go to school the next day in all that humiliation and embarrassment. I was there, but I just barely remember. I remember that Mom cried. I cried, too, but mostly because she did. She was a queenly mountain lady, and she didn't cry much.

I remember everything about Frog Pond Hollar. I only remember seeing Mom cry three other times. She cried when Pearl, our father, picked up a limb and made Ralph, Jewell, and Gladys walk across the Chestuee Creek that ran behind our house while the creek was raging over the banks from a mountain rainstorm. They would have surely drowned had any one of them slipped. They cried, too, but they went across that slippery sycamore foot log to school.

She cried when Dale, my younger brother, was born. But most of all, I remember her crying as she held in her arms Hetty Sue, my baby sister, as she was dying of starvation and pneumonia in a house with no food and no floor. I cried, too.

Oh, yes. She cried one other time. She cried when Pearl, in a drunken stupor, tried to sell Gladys to a Methodist minister and his wife.

Today he would be classified as being socially maladjusted with an alcoholic dependency. We called him a mean drunk. But then we had to live with him, instead of just writing about the subject.

It turned out that the minister's family wanted to take Gladys and raise her. They did, and paid her way to college and graduate school. That's why she has so much more elegance about her than the rest of us. She was raised in a wonderful Methodist minister's parsonage. Gladys is a teacher in Chattanooga now. All of us now have master's degrees or doctorates.

You should have seen us the day they amputated our mother's leg because of arthritis. All eight of us followed her stretcher down the hall to the operating room. There were enough graduate degrees following that little lady who never finished high school to make even the Kennedy family envious.

When I meet Glen Campbell, I'm going to ask him to sing my favorite song of his, and I'm going to dedicate it to Minnie May Morgan Bryson, our Mama. The song: "There Ought to Be a Hall of Fame for Mamas."

If you want the rest of that story, you'll have to read *Team Sponsoring,* or wait until the movie comes out. That may be a while.

In Yellowstone, I was in the beginning stages of formulating how to adapt the Team Sponsoring concept to the church. It is amazing how you are affected by the normal things of life, and how you filter them through your thought processes.

I haven't figured out a way to use that grizzly bear that came roaring across the river as we were all stretched out on a log taking an afternoon siesta.

The only thing I could say about that is, "If you could get your team leaders to move like we did, when that grizzly came toward us, your church would double in a week." I never saw so many hip boots floating down the river as when those fishermen forsook everything and started climbing trees. That's motivation.

But the story I want to tell you is about our visit to the

geysers and mud pots. Earlene and Gladys had been telling us how they look. But Jewell, another brother, the dignified professor who had just retired from a major university in Georgia, said, "You ought to hear them." They had been there before. He then made the sounds of the mud pots. Sounded to me like a cow with a lisp standing there pulling her foot in and out of the mud.

When I saw the field of mud pots and geysers, I yelled, "Looks like my network associates." It looked to me like God had just told a joke. My family helped me pigeonhole each according to church members we all knew. See if any of them fit your group.

Some of the geysers spurted up in the air once a year. Some every month. Some never did spurt; they just sat there and rumbled. Some went off with no degree of regularity; you couldn't tell when they were going to blow their top, but you knew it was coming.

One of the geysers had a beautiful puddle and had a title: Emerald. It looked good, acted good, but never did anything. Just looked good. Isn't that kinda funny? I know people with titles who do nothing.

One mud pot just sat there and fumed, with its only objective in life appearing to be to make a stink. The stench would gag you. Do you know anyone like that? Me, too.

Some of the mud pots just sat there spitting and making an ugly, wheezing, sucking noise, like a team member who had been weaned too late. One geyser just made a rumbling noise. Never did go off. Just sat there and grumbled and rumbled.

I couldn't believe it. If I had tried to imagine a setting that would show off personalities in my group, I could not have found a better setting.

All the geysers and mud pots were not in the same location. When you get your network going, all of yours may not be in the same location either.

Ah, but then they had saved the best until last. The crowds had gathered with an air of expectancy. They knew they were about to see something: "Old Faithful." On the hour she goes off, day in and day out, year in and year out. You can count on her. No surprises. That's the kind of team leader we look for, isn't it? Someone who can be found faithful.

It was fifteen minutes to the airport at Jackson Hole where Ralph and I were to catch our plane back home. But the forest ranger said, "You have to go back out through Idaho; the fire has already jumped the road leading into Jackson Hole." The detour took us a whole day, but what scenery.

"That's our flight they are calling. . . . Bye. See you on board the Holiday next July. See if you can't get Shirley, Wilma, and Ted to save up their money so they can go with us. Jewell, I want you and Ralph to proofread *Networking the Kingdom* as soon as I finish it. I think that's what I'll call it. . . . I'll send it to you. . . . Had a great time. Thanks for everything. . . ."

As our plane soared out over the smoky Grand Tetons, we left behind the beautiful scenery, much of it on fire, taking with us only our memories, dirty clothes, and an almost empty soap tray.

While it was a nearly perfect trip, I had to admit that I was glad to be rid of that plastic bag that I carried my toilet articles and a change of underwear in when I hiked to the "john" in the cold, a block away, and hung it on a nail, when they had one.

Isn't it amazing how you can dislike something so much, even when it's a necessity? That plastic bag is kinda like a bald head. Nobody wants one. But if you had one, you wouldn't take a million dollars for it.

Anyway, I was dreaming, "Boy, I'd pay a dollar for a good hot bath, in a tub. . . ."

But most of all, I couldn't get over how much we would look like those geysers and mud pots, if all but our attitudes and personalities were stripped away. There is probably a little of each of the types in all of us, but I want to become more like "Old Faithful." How 'bout you?

Coda

God gives us a little room and a little broom. When we get that room clean, He gives us a bigger room and a bigger broom.

He said it better though in Matthew 25:21. Let's use His words:

> You did well with small things. So I will let you care for much greater things.
>
> —Matthew 25:21

Duck City

I told my family bye in Jackson Hole. Now I want to say, "Bye" to you, my new kingdom family. My Aunt Zany lives in Ducktown, Tennessee, near Aunt Monnie. But this is a story about Duck City. Our youth director told this beautiful story one Sunday. The original story is by Søren Kierkegaard, the Danish philosopher.

> There was an imaginary city, called Duck City. It had a duck courthouse, a duck mayor, and a duck church. On Sunday mornings the ducks waddled into the church and waddled into their pews.
>
> The duck choir waddled in and sat down. The duck deacons waddled down to the front and sat down. Then the duck minister waddled in and sat down near the duck pulpit.
>
> After the duck ushers received the duck offering, the duck choir arose and quacked out their duck anthem.
>
> Then the duck minister waddled up to the duck pulpit and read from the Duck Bible. He read: "Ducks, you have wings, you can fly like an eagle." The duck congregation yelled, "Amen!"
>
> They had the benediction, and the ducks waddled home.

You have wings, and you can fly. God bless you.

> They shall mount up with wings as eagles: they shall run, and not be weary; and they shall walk, and not faint.
>
> —Isaiah 40:31 (King James Version)

A Blessing

When we started this journey, I told you that I only have words for you. In my way, I said them as well as I could. But I have one thing more to give you. I leave with you "A Rope of Love" that you may begin to tie your new team members to yourself so they won't fall and hurt themselves, and to bind you and them to Jesus the Great Networker as you go on your journey to the kingdom. Don't forget me, and don't forget what I taught you.

O. J. Bryson

21

To Be Continued...

Endnotes

Introduction

1. "O Sacred Head Now Wounded."
2. Hannah Whitall Smith, *The Christian's Secret of a Happy Life* (Old Tappan, N.J.: Fleming H. Revell, 1968).

Chapter 2

1. Evelyn Underhill, *The Spiritual Life* (Moorehouse Publishing Group); reprinted in *A Guide to Prayer* (Nashville: The Upper Room, 1983) pp. 85–86.
2. Hans Kung, *The Church* (New York: Doubleday Books, 1976).

Chapter 6

1. Excerpt from "The Journey of the Magi" in *Collected Poems, 1909–1962* by T. S. Eliot, copyright 1936 by Harcourt Brace

Jovanovich, Inc.; copyright © 1964, 1963 by T. S. Eliot, reprinted by permission of the publisher.

Chapter 8

1. Og Mandino, *The Greatest Salesman in the World* (New York: Bantam Books, 1985) p. 109.

Chapter 11

1. Samuel Moor Shoemaker, "I Stand by the Door," *A Guide to Prayer* (Nashville: The Upper Room, 1983) pp. 305–7; original published by Word, Inc.
2. Elizabeth C. Clephane, "The Ninety and Nine," *The Broadman Hymnal* (Nashville: Broadman Press) p. 36.

Chapter 12

1. Reprinted from *The Prophet* by Kahlil Gibran, by permission of Alfred A. Knopf, Inc.; copyright 1923 by Kahlil Gibran and renewed 1951 by Administrators C.T.A. of Kahlil Gibran Estate and Mary G. Gibran.

Chapter 13

1. C. S. Lewis, *The Weight of Glory* (New York: Macmillan, 1949).

Chapter 14

1. Isaac Watts, "At the Cross."
2. Susan W. N. Ruach, "A New Way of Struggling," *A Guide to Prayer* (Nashville: The Upper Room, 1983) pp. 331–32.
3. Og Mandino, *The Greatest Salesman in the World* (New York: Bantam Books, 1985) p. 90.

Chapter 15

1. Mother Teresa, *A Gift of God* (copyright 1975 by Mother Teresa Missionaries of Charity; New York: Harper & Row).
2. Tennessee Williams.
3. Simon Tugwell, *Prayer* (Springfield IL: Templegate Publications, 1980).
4. Og Mandino, *The Greatest Salesman in the World* (New York: Bantam Books, 1985) flyleaf.
5. Francis of Assisi, from *Our Daily Bread,* quoted in Benjamin R. DeJong, *Uncle Ben's Quotebook* (Eugene, Oreg.: Harvest House, 1976), 160.
6. H. F. Lyte, "Abide with Me."

Chapter 16

1. Carlo Carretto, *Letters from the Desert* (London: Darton, Longman and Todd, 1972).
2. Robert Fulghum, *All I Really Need to Know I Learned in Kindergarten* (New York: Villard Books, 1988) pp. 6–7

Chapter 17

1. Charles Browner, quoted in *Life Is Tremendous,* by Charles "Tremendous" Jones (Wheaton, IL: Tyndale House Publishers, 1981) p. 15.

Chapter 18

1. Dr. James Dobson, *Emotions: Can You Trust Them?* (Ventura, CA: Regal Books, 1980) p. 15.

Chapter 19

1. James Allen, *As a Man Thinketh* (Old Tappan, N.J.: Fleming H. Revell Company).

Appendix

For information on audio and video cassettes, tape of the month, seminars, and so forth, call: ~~281 521 5526~~.

423-842-2474

About the Author

O. J. Bryson, B.A., M.M., D.M.A., is a former university professor with the title: Full Professor with Tenure and Chairman of the Fine Arts Division. His areas of expertise in music are conducting and composition.

Dr. Bryson is from a very humble background. His first house was a shack in the woods with a dirt floor. Originally he is from Frog Pond Hollar, a wooded area about ten miles from Cleveland, Tennessee. He has two sons, Scott and Chris.

He is an internationally known author and speaker. His book, *Team Sponsoring: A Practical Guide To Network Marketing,* is also published in French under the title *Le Parrainage D'Equipes.* It is used in practically every free country in the world where there is network marketing. The publisher is Fleming H. Revell Company.

He has been in the networking business for seven years. To those unfamiliar with networking, this information will have little or no significance. If you are in networking, you will see that his is not the largest nor the smallest network but is rather substantial and rather strong. He is what is called a Diamond. He has a downline Executive Diamond, three Emeralds, several Pearls, Rubies, and about one hundred 25% groups in his total organization.

The U.S.O. sent him and one of his groups, the Heritage Singers, on a six-week tour to Greenland, Iceland, Newfoundland, and Labrador. Concerts Abroad sent his Concert Choir to most major cities of Europe. His group, the Spirit of America Singers, won the Bob Hope Nationwide Talent Search and did the entertainment for six weeks on the Victoria, a luxury ocean liner in the Mediterranean. His groups have performed on national TV with many of the stars.

On university and high school campuses, Dr. Bryson is an often requested speaker to young entrepreneurs. His onstage presentation of the Coffee Shop Meeting, the Coffee Shop Blitz, and the Two-Minute Presentation of networking, which turned the networking business from a "nighttime business to a daytime business," have placed him in the world market as a "can do" speaker in the area of sales, motivation, recruiting, and networking.

His abilities as a storyteller, especially the personal story of his struggle to rise from abject poverty, success over situation, have earned him an affectionate title: the Dream Weaver.